# slow-cooker
# quickfixes

### Recipes for Everyday
### Cover 'n' Cook Convenience

## from the editors of
# Southern Living

©2010 by Time Home Entertainment Inc.
135 West 50th Street, New York, NY 10020

ISBN-10: 0-8487-3351-7
ISBN-13: 978-0-8487-3351-3
Library of Congress Control Number: 2009937189

Printed in the United States of America
First Printing 2010

## Oxmoor House

VP, Publishing Director: Jim Childs
Editorial Director: Susan Payne Dobbs
Brand Manager: Daniel Fagan
Senior Editor: Rebecca Brennan
Managing Editor: Laurie S. Herr

### *Slow-Cooker Quick Fixes*

Editor: Susan Hernandez Ray
Project Editor: Diane Rose
Senior Designer: Melissa Jones Clark
Director, Test Kitchen: Elizabeth Tyler Austin
Assistant Director, Test Kitchen: Julie Christopher
Test Kitchen Professionals: Allison E. Cox, Julie Gunter,
    Kathleen Royal Phillips, Catherine Crowell Steele,
    Ashley T. Strickland
Photography Director: Jim Bathie
Senior Photo Stylist: Kay E. Clarke
Associate Photo Stylist: Katherine Eckert Coyne
Production Manager: Theresa Beste-Farley

## Contributors

Designer: Carol O. Loria
Copy Editor: Donna Baldone
Proofreader: Julie Gillis
Indexer: Mary Ann Laurens
Interns: Georgia Dodge, Perri K. Hubbard, Allison Sperando,
    Christine Taylor

### *Southern Living*®

Executive Editor: Scott Jones
Food Editor: Shannon Sliter Satterwhite
Senior Writer: Donna Florio
Senior Food Editors: Shirley Harrington, Mary Allen Perry
Senior Recipe Editor: Ashley Leath
Assistant Recipe Editor: Ashley Arthur
Test Kitchen Director: Lyda Jones Burnette
Assistant Test Kitchen Director: Rebecca Kracke Gordon
Test Kitchen Specialists/Food Styling: Marian Cooper Cairns,
    Vanessa McNeil Rocchio
Test Kitchen Professionals: Norman King, Pam Lolley, Angela Sellers
Senior Photographers: Ralph Anderson, Jennifer Davick
Photographer: Beth Dreiling Hontzas
Senior Photo Stylist: Buffy Hargett
Editorial Assistant: Pat York

To order additional publications, call 1-800-765-6400 or 1-800-491-0551.

For more books to enrich your life, visit oxmoorhouse.com

To search, savor, and share thousands of recipes, visit myrecipes.com

Cover: (top) Chicken Sausage and White Bean Stew, page 247;
    (bottom) Sesame Chicken, page 91

# {contents}

# Welcome

**Time-pressed cooks** have discovered the marvel of using the slow cooker to create succulent meals with minimal effort. Nothing could be easier than browning some meat, chopping a few ingredients, mixing a little of this and that, and then setting the timer. Then, while the enticing aroma of a home-cooked dinner fills your house, you can go about your day and **come back to a warm, satisfying, fully cooked meal.**

*Slow-Cooker Quick Fixes* **takes the convenience** of the slow cooker up a notch. You'll find top-rated family favorites that can be ready to dish out as you arrive home. And all these recipes can be prepared for the slow cooker in 15 minutes or less. Now that really helps ensure that you spend a minimal amount of time prepping your meals and more time enjoying the delicious results.

Among the book's exciting features are the **"secrets" that let you in on some of our Test Kitchen's favorite hints and tips** for ingredients, slow cookers, great flavor, and much more. And because we understand just how busy you are, we made mealtime even easier by putting together a menu with every recipe. You'll also find a grocery list with each recipe to make your shopping a little bit more simple.

**Happy cooking!**

**Scott Jones**
**Executive Editor**

# slow-cooker savvy

Creating scrumptious meals on your own time is a snap when you use a slow cooker. ✸ Start by selecting the right slow cooker that fits your family size and lifestyle needs. ✸ Next, follow our Test Kitchen's top tips for getting great results every time, and learn a little about slow-cooker safety. ✸ And then discover how easy cleanup can be with a few insider secrets.

# { slow-cooker shopping }

A slow cooker is a cook's best friend. With so many slow cookers on the market, it's hard to know what to buy. Here are some tips to help you get started.

✸ **Size matters.** The first thing to consider when selecting a slow cooker is which best suits your family. If you are cooking for a family of 1 or 2, then a 3- to 4-qt. size should work for you. Families of 4 or larger should look at a 5- or 6-qt. slow cooker. Or, if you love to have leftovers, then a 6-qt. cooker is a good selection.

✸ **Keep a lid on it.** A snug-fitting, see-through lid works best. Removing the cooker's lid during cooking releases a great deal of heat, so you want to be able to see your food through the lid rather than lifting it.

✸ **Removable inserts.** Slow cookers with removable inserts are easier to clean than one-piece units. Depending on the manufacturer, the insert may be dishwasher safe. Some of these inserts can go from the freezer to the cooker, and some can even be used to brown meat on the cooktop before slow cooking.

✸ **It's all in the timing.** Many slow cookers come with programmable timers. This is an especially nice feature if you will be gone all day. If your slow cooker doesn't have one, you can purchase an external timer. Simply plug the external slow-cooker timer into the wall outlet, and then plug the cooker into the timer. It allows you to set your cooking time; when that time has expired, the timer will automatically switch the cooker to warm.

# Follow our Test Kitchen's best tricks.

**1 Make-ahead magic.** If your slow cooker has a removable insert, you can assemble the ingredients in the insert the night before for some recipes, then refrigerate the whole thing. Starting with cold ingredients may increase the cook time.

**2 Don't get burned.** Although cooking time is more flexible in a slow cooker than in an oven, overcooking is possible, so test for doneness close to the time given in the recipe.

**3 Highs and lows.** Some meat recipes call for the dish to be cooked on HIGH heat for 1 hour; then reduced to LOW heat. This allows the slow cooker get the meat to a safe temperature quicker.

**4 Remember time conversions.** One hour on HIGH equals approximately 2 hours on LOW.

**5 Cut uniform pieces.** When cutting meat or vegetables, be sure pieces are the same size so they cook evenly.

**6 Trim the fat.** Slow cooking requires little fat. Trim excess fat and skin from meats and poultry.

**7 Don't stir up things.** There's no need to stir ingredients unless a recipe specifically calls for it. Just layer the ingredients as the recipe directs.

**8 You won't need much liquid.** Use only the amount of liquid specified in a recipe.

**9 Lay it on thick.** You can thicken the juices and make gravy by removing the lid and cooking on HIGH for the last 20 to 30 minutes.

**10 Finish fresh.** Add seasonings and garnishes to the dish once it comes out of the slow cooker to enhance the flavor.

1/3C

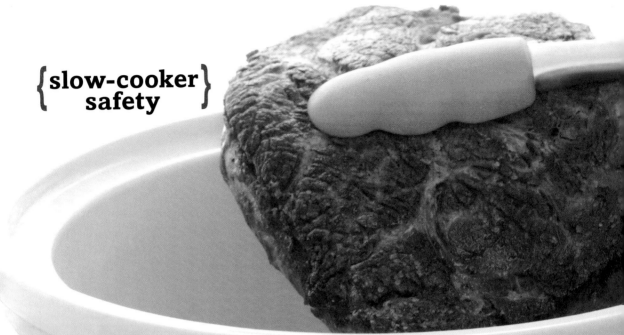

# {slow-cooker safety}

## Slow cooking is a safe method for preparing food if you follow the standard procedures.

✹ Fill your slow cooker at least half full but no more than two-thirds full. This helps meat products reach a safe internal temperature quickly and cook evenly.

✹ The U.S. Department of Agriculture recommends that you cook raw meat and poultry dishes on HIGH for the first hour to speed up the time it takes to reach a safe internal temperature. After the first hour, you can reduce the heat to LOW for the remainder of the cooking time, if desired.

✹ If the recipe calls for browning the meat first, you can forego the HIGH setting for the first hour. Precooking the meat jump-starts the initial temperature of the ingredients, eliminating the safety risk associated with slow cooking raw meats.

✹ Defrost any frozen foods before cooking a dish that includes meat, poultry, or seafood. This ensures that the contents of the insert reach a safe internal temperature quickly.

✹ Don't use your slow cooker to reheat leftovers because the cooker will not heat the food fast enough, resulting in an increased risk of bacterial contamination. Instead, use a microwave or cooktop.

# Follow these tips for making cleaning the slow cooker a little easier.

✳ Allow the slow-cooker insert to cool completely before washing it. Cold water poured over a hot insert can cause it to crack.

✳ To minimize cleanup, buy clear, heavy-duty plastic liners made to fit 3- to 6½-qt. oval and round slow cookers. Place the plastic liner inside the slow cooker before adding the recipe ingredients. Then, serve the meal directly from the slow cooker, with the liner in place. Once the cooker has cooled, just throw away the plastic liner along with the mess.

✳ If you don't have slow-cooker liners, be sure to spray the slow cooker with cooking spray before placing the food inside. This will make cleanup much easier.

✳ The best time to clean the slow cooker is immediately when you take the food out while the slow cooker is still hot. Just make sure that the slow cooker isn't too hot.

✳ Never immerse a slow-cooker unit in water. Simply unplug it and wipe it clean with a cloth.

# meaty suppers

Sit down to home-cooked bliss with this bounty of entrées ranging from meatloaf to lamb chops to pulled pork. ☀ The slow cooker serves up these favorites the way that they are meant to be—juicy, tender, full-flavored, and cooked to perfection. ☀ Topped with robust sauces, flavorful toppings, and vibrant seasonings, this selection of beef, pork, and lamb is a meat lover's delight.

**Shopping Secret: Some stores carry a "fajita mix" of precut vegetables that includes peppers and onions.**

# Pepper Steak With Mushrooms

**hands-on time: 15 min.** • **total time: 8 hr., 25 min.**
**makes 6 servings**

| | |
|---|---|
| 1½ | lb. top round steak |
| 1 | tsp. salt, divided |
| ½ | tsp. pepper, divided |
| 1 | Tbsp. vegetable oil |
| 3 | cups presliced green, yellow, and red bell pepper mix |
| 2 | garlic cloves, minced |
| 1 | medium onion, vertically sliced |
| 1 | (14½-oz.) can diced tomatoes with basil, garlic, and oregano |
| 1 | (8-oz.) package sliced baby portobello mushrooms |
| 1 | (10½-oz.) can beef consommé |
| 2 | Tbsp. soy sauce |
| 2 | Tbsp. tomato paste |
| 2 | Tbsp. cornstarch |

**1.** Cut beef diagonally across the grain into thin slices. Sprinkle beef with ¾ tsp. salt and ¼ tsp. pepper. Heat oil in a large nonstick skillet over medium-high heat. Cook beef in hot oil, stirring frequently, 6 to 8 minutes or until browned; drain. Place beef in a 5-qt. slow cooker. Add bell peppers and next 4 ingredients to slow cooker. Toss gently.

**2.** Whisk together consommé, soy sauce, tomato paste, and remaining ¼ tsp. each salt and pepper; stir into beef mixture. Cover and cook on LOW 8 hours or until beef is very tender.

**3.** Whisk together cornstarch and 2 Tbsp. water; gradually stir into liquid in slow cooker. Cover and cook on HIGH 10 minutes or until thickened. Serve over mashed potatoes.

# Grillades and Cheese Grits

hands-on time: 15 min. • total time: 6 hr., 30 min.
makes 6 servings

2     lb. top round steak (about ½ inch thick)
1     tsp. salt, divided
¼     tsp. pepper
¼     cup all-purpose flour, divided
2     Tbsp. vegetable oil
2     (8-oz.) containers refrigerated prechopped celery, onion, and
      bell pepper mix
3     garlic cloves, minced
1     (14-oz.) can beef broth
1     tsp. dried Italian seasoning
½     tsp. ground red pepper
2     (14.5-oz.) cans diced tomatoes with basil, garlic, and oregano
2     cups uncooked quick-cooking grits
2     cups (8 oz.) Gruyère cheese, shredded
Garnish: chopped fresh parsley

**1.** Sprinkle steak with ½ tsp. salt and pepper. Set aside 1 Tbsp. flour. Cut steak into 2-inch pieces; dredge in remaining flour.

**2.** Heat oil in a large nonstick skillet over medium-high heat; add steak, and cook 3 minutes on each side or until browned. Transfer to a 5-qt. slow cooker. Add celery mix and garlic to skillet; sauté 3 minutes. Add beef broth, stirring to loosen particles from bottom. Stir in Italian seasoning and red pepper. Pour mixture over steak. Drain 1 can tomatoes. Add drained tomatoes and remaining can tomatoes to steak mixture. Cover and cook on LOW 6 hours or until steak is very tender.

**3.** Increase heat to HIGH. Stir together reserved flour and 2 Tbsp. water until smooth; gently stir into steak mixture. Cover and cook 15 minutes or until mixture is slightly thickened.

**4.** Meanwhile, bring 8 cups water and remaining ½ tsp. salt to a boil in a 4-qt. saucepan; gradually whisk in grits. Reduce heat, and simmer, whisking often, 5 minutes or until thickened; stir in cheese. Serve grillades over grits. Garnish, if desired.

## ideal slow cooker:
### 5-quart

## menu idea
### for 6

**Grillades and Cheese Grits**

**Steamed asparagus**

## groceries needed...

Check staples: salt, pepper, flour, vegetable oil, dried Italian seasoning, ground red pepper

* 2 lb. top round steak
* 2 (8-oz.) containers refrigerated prechopped celery, onion, and bell pepper mix
* 1 garlic bulb
* 1 (14-oz.) can beef broth
* 2 (14.5-oz.) cans diced tomatoes with basil, garlic, and oregano
* 1 package quick-cooking grits
* 2 cups (8 oz.) Gruyère cheese
* 1 bunch fresh parsley

## side...

* 1 lb. fresh asparagus

*groceries needed...*

Check staples: jarred minced garlic, flour, salt, ground pepper, Worcestershire sauce, dried Italian seasoning

- 1 package bacon
- 2 (8-oz.) containers refrigerated prechopped celery, onion, and bell pepper mix
- 1¼ lb. bottom round steak
- 1 (14-oz.) can beef broth
- 1 (14.5-oz.) can diced fire-roasted tomatoes

*sides...*

- 1 (24-oz.) package refrigerated mashed potatoes
- 1 lb. green beans

# Swiss Steak

**hands-on time: 15 min.** • **total time: 8 hr., 15 min.**
**makes 4 servings**

| | |
|---|---|
| 5 | bacon slices, halved |
| 2 | (8-oz.) containers refrigerated prechopped celery, onion, and bell pepper mix |
| 2 | Tbsp. jarred minced garlic |
| 1¼ | lb. bottom round steak (about 1 inch thick), cut into 4 equal portions |
| ⅓ | cup all-purpose flour |
| 1½ | tsp. salt |
| ¾ | tsp. freshly ground pepper |
| 1 | (14-oz.) can beef broth |
| 1 | (14.5-oz.) can diced fire-roasted tomatoes, undrained |
| 1 | Tbsp. Worcestershire sauce |
| 1 | tsp. dried Italian seasoning |

**1.** Cook bacon in a large nonstick skillet over medium-high heat 5 to 6 minutes or until crisp; remove bacon, and drain on paper towels, reserving drippings in skillet. Crumble bacon; set aside. Cook celery mix and garlic in hot drippings, stirring often, until tender. Transfer vegetables to a 5-qt. slow cooker, using a slotted spoon. Reserve drippings in pan.

**2.** While vegetables cook, place meat on a sheet of plastic wrap, and flatten with the pointed side of a meat mallet until ¼-inch thickness. Combine flour, salt, and pepper in a shallow dish. Dredge meat in flour mixture; cook in hot drippings 3 minutes on each side or until browned.

**3.** Place meat in slow cooker over vegetables, reserving drippings in skillet. Add beef broth and remaining ingredients to skillet stirring to loosen particles from bottom. Pour broth mixture over beef in slow cooker. Cover and cook on LOW 8 hours or until beef is very tender. Sprinkle with crumbled bacon before serving.

# Beef With Olives

hands-on time: 15 min. • total time: 5 hr., 15 min.
makes 8 to 10 servings

¼ cup butter, melted

3 lb. boneless top sirloin steak, cut into 1½-inch pieces

¼ tsp. salt

½ tsp. pepper

1 Tbsp. olive oil

3 large garlic cloves, sliced

2 shallots, vertically sliced

2 cups pimiento-stuffed Spanish olives

2 Tbsp. olive juice from jar

1 (12-oz.) jar roasted red bell peppers, drained and cut into thick strips

**1.** Pour melted butter into a 4- or 5-qt. slow cooker.

**2.** Sprinkle beef with salt and pepper. Heat oil in a large skillet over medium-high heat. Cook beef, in 2 batches, 2 minutes on each side. Place beef in slow cooker. Add garlic and shallots to skillet; sauté 1 minute over medium-high heat. Spoon over beef in slow cooker. Coarsely chop 1 cup olives. Sprinkle chopped and whole olives and olive juice over beef.

**3.** Cover and cook on LOW 5 hours or until beef is tender. Stir in roasted bell peppers just before serving.

*ideal slow cooker:*
4- or 5-quart

*menu idea*
**for 8 to 10**

Beef With Olives

Hot cooked yellow rice

Tossed salad

*groceries needed...*

- Check staples: butter, salt, pepper, olive oil, salad dressing
- 3 lb. boneless top sirloin steak
- 1 garlic bulb
- 2 shallots
- 1 (12-oz.) jar pimiento-stuffed Spanish olives
- 1 (12-oz.) jar roasted red bell peppers

*sides...*

- 1 (16-oz.) bag yellow rice
- 1 head iceberg lettuce

## ideal slow cooker:

### 5-quart

## menu idea

### for 6 to 8

Cranberry
Corned Beef

Steamed
Brussels sprouts

## groceries needed...

Check staples: black pepper

* 1 (4-lb.) cured corned beef brisket with spice packet
* 1 lb. carrots
* 1 large onion
* 1 (14-oz.) can whole-berry cranberry sauce
* 1 (14-oz.) can jellied cranberry sauce
* 2 (1-oz.) envelopes dry onion soup mix
* 1 (8-oz.) container sour cream
* 1 (5-oz.) jar refrigerated horseradish
* 1 bunch fresh parsley

## side...

* 1½ lb. Brussels sprouts

**Ingredient Secret:** A typical corned beef brisket comes with a small spice packet tucked inside. Be careful not to discard the packet; it adds a layer of flavor to the meat as it slow cooks.

# Cranberry Corned Beef

**hands-on time: 12 min.** • **total time: 9 hr., 12 min.**
**makes 6 to 8 servings**

| | |
|---|---|
| 1 | (4-lb.) cured corned beef brisket with spice packet |
| 5 | large carrots, cut into 3-inch pieces |
| 1 | large onion, cut into 6 wedges |
| 1 | (14-oz.) can whole-berry cranberry sauce |
| 1 | (14-oz.) can jellied cranberry sauce |
| 2 | (1-oz.) envelopes dry onion soup mix |
| ½ | cup sour cream |
| 4 | tsp. refrigerated horseradish |
| ¼ | tsp. freshly ground black pepper |

Garnish: chopped fresh parsley

**1.** Trim fat from brisket. Place carrot and onion in a 5-qt. slow cooker; place brisket on top of vegetables. Sprinkle spice packet seasonings over brisket.

**2.** Combine cranberry sauces and soup mix. Spoon over brisket. Cover and cook on HIGH 1 hour. Reduce heat to LOW, and cook 8 hours.

**3.** Meanwhile, combine sour cream and horseradish in a small bowl. Cover and chill until ready to serve.

**4.** Transfer brisket to a serving platter. Spoon carrot, onion, and, if desired, a little cooking liquid around brisket on platter. Stir pepper into sour-cream horseradish sauce. Serve with sauce. Sprinkle with pepper. Garnish, if desired.

# Beef Brisket Soft Tacos

hands-on time: 15 min. • total time: 6 hr., 15 min.
makes 6 to 8 servings

2    medium onions, thinly sliced
2    celery ribs, thinly sliced
2    garlic cloves, pressed
1    (2-lb.) beef brisket
2    tsp. salt
1½   tsp. ground chipotle powder
1    cup coarsely chopped fresh cilantro
10   (8-inch) flour tortillas
Toppings: shredded Mexican cheese blend, sour cream, salsa,
     chopped fresh cilantro
Lime wedges

1. Place first 3 ingredients in a 6-qt. slow cooker.

2. Trim fat from brisket; cut brisket into 3-inch pieces. Rub brisket pieces with 2 tsp. salt and 1½ tsp. chipotle powder, and place on top of vegetables in slow cooker. Top with 1 cup cilantro.

3. Cover and cook on HIGH 6 hours or until brisket pieces shred easily with a fork.

4. Remove brisket from slow cooker, and cool slightly. Using 2 forks, shred meat into bite-size pieces. Return mixture to slow cooker. Serve in flour tortillas with desired toppings and lime wedges.

*menu idea*
for 6 to 8

Beef Brisket
Soft Tacos

Black beans

*groceries needed...*

Check staples: salt

❋ 2 medium onions
❋ 1 bunch celery
❋ 1 garlic bulb
❋ 1 (2-lb.) beef brisket
❋ 1 bottle chipotle powder
❋ 1 bunch fresh cilantro
❋ 1 (10-count) package (8-inch) flour tortillas
❋ 1 (16-oz.) package shredded Mexican cheese blend
❋ 1 (16-oz.) container sour cream
❋ 1 (16-oz.) jar salsa
❋ 2 limes

*side...*
❋ 2 (15-oz.) cans black beans

*menu idea*
**for 6**

**Cowboy Pot Roast**

**Tortilla chips**

*groceries needed...*

Check staples: salt, pepper,
chili powder, vegetable oil

* 1 (14.5-oz.) can petite-cut diced
  tomatoes
* 1 (10-oz.) can diced tomatoes and
  green chiles
* 1 onion
* 1 (2½- to 3-lb.) eye of round roast
* 2 (16-oz.) cans pinto beans
* 1 (15-oz.) can black beans
* 1 jar of pickled jalapeño pepper
  slices (optional)

*side...*

* 1 package tortilla chips

# Cowboy Pot Roast

**hands-on time: 15 min.  ·  total time: 8 hr., 45 min.**
**makes 6 servings**

1½  tsp. salt, divided

1½  tsp. pepper, divided

1  (14.5-oz.) can petite-cut diced tomatoes, drained

1  (10-oz.) can diced tomatoes and green chiles, undrained

1  onion, cut into 8 wedges

1  Tbsp. chili powder

1  (2½- to 3-lb.) eye of round roast, trimmed

2  Tbsp. vegetable oil

2  (16-oz.) cans pinto beans, drained

1  (15-oz.) can black beans, drained

Pickled jalapeño pepper slices (optional)

1. Combine 1 tsp. salt, 1 tsp. pepper, and next 4 ingredients in a medium bowl. Sprinkle roast with remaining ½ tsp. salt and ½ tsp. pepper. Brown roast on all sides in hot oil in a large Dutch oven over medium-high heat. Transfer roast to a 5-qt. slow cooker. Pour tomato mixture over roast. Cover and cook on LOW for 8 to 10 hours or until very tender.

2. Remove roast from slow cooker, and cut into large chunks; keep warm.

3. Skim fat from juices in slow cooker. Mash 1½ cans (about 2¾ cups) pinto beans; add to slow cooker, and stir until combined. Stir in black beans and remaining ½ can pinto beans. Add roast pieces back to slow cooker; cover and cook on HIGH 20 minutes more. Top each serving with jalapeño pepper slices, if desired.

## Spicy Shredded Beef Sandwiches

hands-on time: 5 min. • total time: 9 hr., 5 min.
makes 6 to 8 servings

1    (2½ lb.) boneless chuck roast, trimmed

1    (14½-oz.) can diced tomatoes, undrained

1    (7-oz.) can adobo sauce or 1 (7-oz.) jar spicy salsa

1    (4-oz.) can jalapeño peppers, drained

1    (8-oz.) container refrigerated prechopped onion (about 1¾ cups)

1½  tsp. jarred minced garlic

2    Tbsp. chili powder

1    Tbsp. honey

2½  tsp. kosher salt

1    tsp. ground cumin

2    cups beef broth

Crusty French rolls

Toppings: shredded cabbage, sliced red onion, sliced tomato, sour cream, chopped cilantro

1. Place beef in a 5-qt. slow cooker. Add tomatoes, adobo sauce, jalapeños, onion, garlic, chili powder, honey, salt, and cumin; pour broth over the top.

2. Cover and cook on HIGH 1 hour; reduce heat to LOW, and cook 8 hours. If desired, remove lid during last 30 minutes to allow sauce to reduce and thicken.

3. With a heavy fork, transfer meat to a rimmed board or plate. Shred with two forks. Ladle out half the sauce and reserve (see Serving Secret above.) Return shredded beef to the remaining sauce in slow cooker; cover and keep warm. Serve on rolls. Add desired toppings.

ideal slow cooker:
5-quart

### menu idea
#### for 6 to 8

Spicy Shredded Beef Sandwiches

Sweet potato fries

### groceries needed...

Check staples: jarred minced garlic, chili powder, honey, kosher salt, cumin

* 2½ lb. boneless chuck roast
* 1 (14½-oz.) can diced tomatoes
* 1 (7-oz.) can adobo sauce or 1 (7-oz.) jar spicy salsa
* 1 (4-oz.) can diced jalapeño peppers
* 1 (8-oz.) container refrigerated prechopped onion
* 2 (14-oz.) cans beef broth
* 1 package French rolls
* 1 package shredded cabbage
* 1 red onion
* 1 tomato
* 1 (8-oz.) container sour cream
* 1 bunch cilantro

### side...
* 1 (20-oz.) package sweet potato fries

*menu idea*
### for 6 to 8

**Beef Stroganoff**

**Egg noodles**

**Iceberg lettuce wedges with cherry tomatoes**

*groceries needed...*

Check staples: flour, salt, pepper, olive oil, Dijon mustard, salad dressing

* 2 lb. beef sirloin tips
* 2 medium onions
* 2 (8-oz.) packages sliced fresh mushrooms
* 1 (14-oz.) can beef broth
* 1 (6-oz.) can tomato paste
* 1 (16-oz.) container sour cream
* 1 bottle dry sherry (optional)
* 1 bunch parsley (optional)

*sides...*

* 1 (16-oz.) package egg noodles
* 1 head iceberg lettuce
* 1 pt. cherry tomatoes

# Beef Stroganoff

hands-on time: 15 min. • total time: 3 hr., 15 min.
makes 6 to 8 servings

¼  cup all-purpose flour
2  lb. beef sirloin tips
½  tsp. salt
½  tsp. freshly ground pepper
2  Tbsp. olive oil
2  medium onions, chopped
2  (8-oz.) packages sliced fresh mushrooms
1½  cups beef broth
2  Tbsp. tomato paste
1  Tbsp. Dijon mustard
1½  cups sour cream
¼  cup dry sherry (optional)
**Hot cooked egg noodles**
**Chopped fresh parsley (optional)**

1. Place flour in a shallow dish. Sprinkle beef with salt and pepper; dredge in flour. Heat a large skillet over medium-high heat; add oil. Add beef; cook 7 minutes or until browned, stirring occasionally. Transfer to a greased 5-qt. slow cooker. Add onion and mushrooms to drippings in skillet; cook, stirring often, 3 minutes or until tender.

2. Meanwhile, combine broth, tomato paste, and mustard. Add broth mixture to skillet, stirring to loosen particles from bottom of skillet. Pour over beef in slow cooker.

3. Cover and cook on LOW 3 hours or until beef is tender. Just before serving, stir in sour cream and, if desired, sherry. Serve over noodles. Sprinkle with parsley, if desired.

**Slow-Cooker Secret: Using an oval slow cooker helps maintain the traditional meatloaf shape.**

# Homestyle Meatloaf

**hands-on time: 11 min.** • **total time: 4 hr., 36 min.**
**makes 8 servings**

2   Tbsp. butter
1   (8-oz.) container refrigerated prechopped celery, onion, and bell pepper mix
2   garlic cloves, minced
2   lb. ground round
¾   cup uncooked quick-cooking oats
1   cup ketchup, divided
¾   tsp. salt
½   tsp. freshly ground pepper
2   large eggs, lightly beaten
2   Tbsp. brown sugar
1   Tbsp. yellow mustard

**1.** Melt butter in a large skillet over medium-high heat. Add celery mixture and garlic; sauté 3 minutes or until tender. Combine sautéed mixture, ground round, oats, ½ cup ketchup, salt, pepper, and eggs in a large bowl.

**2.** Shape mixture into a 9- x 4-inch loaf; place in a lightly greased 5- or 6-qt. oval slow cooker.

**3.** Cover and cook on HIGH 1 hour. Reduce heat to LOW, and cook 3 more hours. Remove slow cooker insert, and carefully pour off excess fat. Return insert to cooker.

**4.** Stir together remaining ½ cup ketchup, brown sugar, and mustard. Spread over meatloaf. Cover and cook on LOW 15 minutes or until no longer pink in center. Remove meatloaf from insert, and let stand 10 minutes before serving.

*menu idea*
**for 8**

Homestyle Meatloaf
Mashed potatoes
Green beans

*groceries needed...*

Check staples: butter, ketchup, salt, pepper, eggs, brown sugar, mustard

* 1 (8-oz.) container refrigerated prechopped celery, onion, and bell pepper mix
* 1 garlic bulb
* 2 lb. ground round
* 1 container quick-cooking oats

*sides...*

* 1 (24-oz.) package refrigerated mashed potatoes
* 2 lb. fresh green beans

*menu idea*

**for 4**

**Beef Ragu With Penne**

**Crusty French bread**

**Salad**

*groceries needed...*

Check staples: kosher salt, black pepper, salad dressing

* 1 large onion
* 2 lb. ground beef
* 2 (28-oz.) cans crushed tomatoes
* 1 (16-oz.) package penne
* 1 container finely grated Parmesan cheese
* 1 bunch fresh basil

*sides...*

* 1 bag prewashed lettuce
* 1 box of croutons
* 1 loaf French bread

**Substitution Secret: You can substitute gemelli pasta, cellentani pasta, or macaroni for the penne.**

# Beef Ragu With Penne

**hands-on time: 8 min. • total time: 4 hr., 8 min.**
**makes 4 servings**

1    large onion, chopped
2    lb. ground beef
2    (28-oz.) cans crushed tomatoes
1    tsp. kosher salt
1    (16-oz.) package penne pasta
¼    cup finely grated Parmesan cheese
2    Tbsp. chopped fresh basil
Freshly ground black pepper to taste

1. Place onion in a 5-qt. slow cooker. Crumble ground beef over onion, and add tomatoes. Cover and cook for 4 hours on HIGH or 8 hours on LOW. Break up any large pieces of beef with a wooden spoon. Add salt. Remove half of sauce, and reserve for another use; keep remaining sauce warm in slow cooker.

2. Cook pasta according to package directions, stirring often. Drain and transfer to 4 shallow bowls. Spoon meat sauce over each portion of pasta. Serve with Parmesan cheese, basil, and freshly ground pepper.

**Slow-Cooker Secret:** A common mistake in cooking rice from scratch is to add too much liquid, which can make it gummy. There's not a lot of liquid in this recipe to start with, but the tomatoes and vegetables produce just enough to steam the rice.

# Slow-Cooked Cajun Dirty Rice

hands-on time: 10 min. • total time: 2 hr., 10 min.
makes 8 servings

1    lb. lean ground beef
1    lb. ground pork sausage
2    tsp. Cajun seasoning
2    (8-oz.) containers refrigerated prechopped celery, onion, and bell pepper mix
2    cups uncooked converted long-grain rice
¼    tsp. ground red pepper
1    (10-oz.) can diced tomatoes with green chiles, undrained
1    cup chicken broth

1. Brown first 3 ingredients in a large skillet over medium-high heat, stirring often, 8 minutes or until meat crumbles and is no longer pink. Transfer meat mixture to a 5-qt. slow cooker, using a slotted spoon.

2. Stir in celery mix and remaining ingredients. Cover and cook on LOW 2 hours or until liquid is absorbed and rice is tender.

*ideal slow cooker:*
5-quart

*menu idea*
for 8

Slow-Cooked
Cajun Dirty Rice
Cornbread

*groceries needed...*
Check staples: Cajun seasoning, ground red pepper
* 1 lb. lean ground beef
* 1 lb. ground pork sausage
* 2 (8-oz.) containers refrigerated prechopped celery, onion, and bell pepper mix
* 1 box converted long-grain rice
* 1 (10-oz.) can diced tomatoes with green chiles
* 1 (14-oz.) can chicken broth

*side...*
* Deli cornbread

## groceries needed...

Check staples: olive oil, salt, pepper, milk, nutmeg

- 2 (8-oz.) containers refrigerated prechopped celery, onion, and bell pepper mix
- 1 bunch carrots
- 1 garlic bulb
- 1½ lb. ground chuck
- 1 bottle dry white wine
- 1 (28-oz.) can whole San Marzano tomatoes in tomato purée, undrained and chopped
- 12 oz. pappardelle pasta
- 1 container freshly grated Parmesan cheese (optional)
- 1 bunch parsley (optional)

## side...

- 2 (11.4-oz.) packages Caesar salad kit

**Ingredient Secret: Pappardelle is pasta shaped like wide ribbons. If your store doesn't stock it, you may substitute the more narrow fettuccine, or, narrower still, tagliatelle.**

# Pappardelle Bolognese

**hands-on time: 15 min.** • **total time: 6 hr., 15 min.**
**makes 6 servings**

2    Tbsp. olive oil

2    cups refrigerated prechopped celery, onion, and bell pepper mix

½    cup chopped carrot

2    garlic cloves, pressed

1½   lb. ground chuck

¾    tsp. salt

¾    tsp. freshly ground pepper

2    cups milk

1½   cups dry white wine

¼    tsp. freshly ground nutmeg

1    (28-oz.) can whole San Marzano tomatoes in tomato purée, undrained and chopped

Hot cooked pappardelle pasta

Freshly grated Parmesan cheese (optional)

Chopped fresh parsley (optional)

1. Heat oil in a large nonstick skillet over medium-high heat. Add celery mixture and carrot; sauté 3 minutes or until tender. Add garlic; sauté 1 minute. Transfer vegetable mixture to a lightly greased 5-qt. slow cooker.

2. Add beef, salt, and pepper to pan; cook 5 minutes, stirring until beef crumbles and is no longer pink. Add beef mixture to vegetable mixture. Stir in milk and next 3 ingredients.

3. Cover and cook on HIGH 6 hours. Serve sauce over hot cooked pasta; sprinkle with Parmesan cheese and parsley, if desired.

# Shortcut Ravioli Lasagna

hands-on time: 15 min. • total time: 6 hr., 23 min.
makes 4 to 6 servings

1   lb. ground round
1   cup refrigerated prechopped onion
2   garlic cloves, minced (optional)
1   (24-oz.) jar pasta sauce
1   (25-oz.) package frozen cheese-filled ravioli (do not thaw)
1   (8-oz.) package shredded Italian six-cheese blend

1. Cook ground round, onion, and, if desired, garlic in a large skillet over medium-high heat until beef crumbles and is no longer pink. Drain, if needed.

2. Spoon ¾ cup pasta sauce into bottom of a lightly greased 4-qt. slow cooker. Layer half of ravioli, half of meat mixture, and 1 cup cheese over sauce. Repeat layers with ¾ cup sauce, remaining ravioli, and remaining meat mixture. Top with remaining sauce; sprinkle with remaining 1 cup cheese.

3. Cover and cook on LOW 6 hours or until pasta is tender.

*menu idea*
### for 6

**Swedish Meatballs**

**Hot cooked medium egg noodles**

**Peas and carrots**

*groceries needed...*

Check staples: vegetable oil, flour, salt, garlic powder, pepper, nutmeg

* 1 (32-oz.) package frozen fully cooked meatballs (we tested with Farm Rich)
* 1 (14-oz.) can chicken broth
* 1 bottle dry white wine
* 1 (8-oz.) container sour cream
* 1 bunch fresh parsley
* 1 (8-oz.) jar red currant jelly (optional)

*sides...*

* 1 (12-oz.) bag egg noodles
* 2 (10-oz.) packages frozen peas and carrots

# Swedish Meatballs

**hands-on time: 14 min.** • **total time: 3 hr., 14 min.**
**makes 6 servings**

| 1 | (32-oz.) package frozen fully cooked meatballs |
| 2 | Tbsp. vegetable oil |
| ¼ | cup all-purpose flour |
| ½ | tsp. salt |
| ¼ | tsp. garlic powder |
| ¼ | tsp. freshly ground pepper |
| ⅛ | tsp. ground nutmeg |
| 2 | cups chicken broth |
| ½ | cup white wine |
| ½ | cup sour cream |
| 2 | Tbsp. chopped fresh parsley |
| ½ | cup red currant jelly (optional) |

**Hot cooked noodles**

**Garnish: chopped fresh parsley**

**1.** Cook meatballs in a large skillet over medium-high heat 5 minutes turning occasionally until browned on all sides.

**2.** Place meatballs in a 4-qt. slow cooker, reserving drippings in skillet. Reduce heat to low; add oil to skillet. Whisk in flour and next 4 ingredients until smooth. Increase heat to medium; cook, whisking constantly, 1 minute. Gradually whisk in chicken broth and wine. Cook, whisking frequently, 4 minutes or until slightly thickened. Pour gravy over meatballs. Cover and cook 3 hours on LOW.

**3.** Remove meatballs from slow cooker with a slotted spoon, and place in a serving bowl. Add sour cream, parsley, and, if desired, jelly to gravy, whisking until blended. Pour over meatballs. Serve over hot cooked noodles; garnish, if desired.

**Shopping Secret:** Garam masala is a blend of Indian spices that are also found in North African, specifically Moroccan, dishes. Using a spice blend reduces the number of individual spices to purchase and measure for this recipe.

# Fruited Lamb Tagine

hands-on time: 15 min. • total time: 8 hr., 15 min.
makes 4 servings

| | |
|---|---|
| 2 | Tbsp. all-purpose flour |
| 2 | tsp. garam masala |
| ½ | tsp. ground turmeric |
| ½ | tsp. salt |
| ¼ | tsp. pepper |
| 2 | lb. boneless leg of lamb, cut into 1½-inch cubes |
| 2 | Tbsp. olive oil |
| 1 | (8-oz.) container refrigerated prechopped onion |
| 1 | (14-oz.) can beef broth |
| 1 | cup dried pitted plums |
| 1 | cup dried apricots |
| ⅓ | cup orange marmalade |

Garnishes: chopped fresh cilantro, toasted slivered almonds

1. Combine first 5 ingredients in a large zip-top plastic freezer bag; add lamb. Seal bag, shaking to coat.

2. Heat oil in a large skillet over medium-high heat until hot; add lamb. Cook 2 minutes on each side or until browned.

3. Place lamb and onion in a 4- to 5-qt. slow cooker. Add broth and next 3 ingredients, stirring well. Cover and cook on LOW 8 hours or until meat is very tender. Garnish, if desired.

*ideal slow cooker:*
4- or 5-quart

*menu idea*
for 4

**Fruited Lamb Tagine**
**Couscous**
**Roasted carrots**

*groceries needed...*

Check staples: flour, salt, pepper, olive oil

* 1 (1.8-oz.) jar garam masala
* 1 (1.6-oz.) jar ground turmeric
* 2 lb. boneless leg of lamb
* 1 (8-oz.) container refrigerated prechopped onion
* 1 (14-oz.) can beef broth
* 1 (6-oz.) package dried pitted plums
* 1 (6-oz.) package dried apricots
* 1 (12-oz.) jar orange marmalade
* 1 bunch fresh cilantro (optional)
* 1 package slivered almonds (optional)

*sides...*

* 1 (6.3-oz.) box couscous
* 1 bunch carrots

*menu idea*

**for 8 to 10**

**Garlicky
Leg of Lamb Over
Feta Potatoes**

**Peas**

*groceries needed...*

Check staples: kosher salt, coarsely ground pepper, olive oil, balsamic vinegar

- 1 (4-lb.) boneless leg of lamb
- 1 garlic bulb
- 1 (10.5-oz.) jar red pepper jelly
- 1 bunch fresh mint
- 2 (24-oz.) packages refrigerated mashed potatoes
- 2 (4-oz.) containers feta cheese
- 1 lemon

*side...*

- 2 (10-oz.) packages frozen peas

# Garlicky Leg of Lamb Over Feta Potatoes

**hands-on time: 13 min.** • **total time: 8 hr., 13 min.**
**makes 8 to 10 servings**

| | |
|---|---|
| 1 | (4-lb.) boneless leg of lamb, trimmed |
| 8 | large garlic cloves, crushed |
| 2 | tsp. kosher salt |
| 1½ | tsp. coarsely ground pepper, divided |
| 2 | Tbsp. olive oil |
| ¾ | cup red pepper jelly |
| ¼ | cup chopped fresh mint |
| 2 | Tbsp. balsamic vinegar |
| 2 | (24-oz.) packages refrigerated mashed potatoes |
| 6 | oz. feta cheese, crumbled |
| 1½ | tsp. lemon zest |

**Garnishes: minced fresh mint, lemon zest**

**1.** Roll up lamb, and tie with string at 2- to 3-inch intervals. Peel and slice cloves in half lengthwise. Cut 16 slits (about ½-inch deep) into lamb; insert a garlic piece into each slit. Rub salt and 1 tsp. pepper all over lamb.

**2.** Heat oil in a large skillet over medium-high heat. Sear lamb 5 minutes, turning twice with tongs. Place lamb in a lightly greased 5-qt. slow cooker.

**3.** Combine pepper jelly, next 2 ingredients, and remaining ½ tsp. pepper; stir until melted. Pour over lamb. Cover and cook on LOW 8 hours or until lamb is very tender.

**4.** Near the end of cook time, cook 1 package potatoes 3 minutes in microwave according to package directions. Stir potatoes; stir in half of cheese. Cook 3 more minutes. Stir in ¾ tsp. lemon zest. Repeat procedure with remaining potatoes, cheese, and lemon zest.

**5.** Remove string, and carve lamb; serve with potatoes. Garnish, if desired.

> **Ingredient Secret:** Greek seasoning is a mixture of oregano, mint, garlic, onion, black pepper, and lemon zest.

*ideal slow cooker:*
**5-quart**

# Braised Rosemary Lamb Chops

**hands-on time: 13 min.** • **total time: 6 hr., 13 min.**
**makes 4 servings**

| | |
|---|---|
| 4 | lamb shoulder chops |
| 4 | tsp. Greek seasoning |
| 2 | Tbsp. olive oil |
| 1 | (8-oz.) container refrigerated prechopped celery, onion, and bell pepper mix |
| 1 | cup chicken broth |
| ¼ | cup chopped drained sun-dried tomatoes in oil |
| 1 | tsp. chopped fresh rosemary |
| ¼ | tsp. chili powder |
| 1 | (16-oz.) can garbanzo beans, drained |
| 1 | (14-oz.) can artichoke hearts, drained |

Hot cooked couscous

Pine nuts, toasted

Garnish: lemon zest

**1.** Rub lamb chops on both sides with Greek seasoning. Heat oil in a medium skillet over medium-high heat. Add lamb; cook 3 minutes on each side or until browned.

**2.** Place lamb in a 5-qt. slow cooker, reserving drippings in skillet. Cook celery mix in hot drippings 2 minutes. Remove pan from heat. Add chicken broth, and next 3 ingredients to pan, stirring to loosen browned bits.

**3.** Add beans and artichoke hearts to slow cooker. Pour broth mixture over lamb and vegetables. Cover and cook on LOW 6 hours or until lamb is tender. Spoon lamb and vegetables over couscous, using a slotted spoon. Sprinkle with pine nuts, and garnish with lemon zest, if desired.

*menu idea*
**for 4**

**Braised Rosemary Lamb Chops**

**Couscous**

**Greek salad**

*groceries needed...*

Check staples: Greek seasoning (we tested with Cavender's), olive oil, chili powder

* 4 lamb shoulder chops
* 1 (8-oz.) container refrigerated prechopped celery, onion, and bell pepper mix
* 1 (14-oz.) can chicken broth
* 1 jar sun-dried tomatoes in oil
* 1 bunch fresh rosemary
* 1 (16-oz.) can garbanzo beans
* 1 (14-oz.) can artichoke hearts
* 1 (10-oz.) box plain couscous
* 1 container pine nuts
* 1 lemon

*side...*

* 1 Greek salad kit

menu idea

for 4

Veal Chops With
Figs

Risotto

Mashed butternut
squash

groceries needed...

Check staples: sugar, coarsely ground
or freshly ground pepper, olive oil,
balsamic vinegar

- 1 (16-oz.) bottle pomegranate juice
- 1 garlic bulb
- 1 bunch fresh thyme
- 4 (1- to 1½-inch-thick) veal rib
  chops
- 2 shallots
- 1 (8-oz.) package dried figs

sides...

- 1 (9.9-oz.) package risotto
- 1 butternut squash

Ingredient Secret: We tested this recipe
using veal rib chops, but loin chops
would work as well. The thicker the
better here, since the meat simmers
low and slow to melt-in-your-mouth
tenderness.

# Veal Chops With Figs

hands-on time: 15 min. • total time: 6 hr., 15 min.
makes 4 servings

1    cup pomegranate juice
¾    cup sugar
6    garlic cloves, minced
1    Tbsp. chopped fresh thyme
1    tsp. coarsely ground or freshly ground pepper
4    (1- to 1½-inch-thick) veal rib chops
1    Tbsp. olive oil
2    shallots, vertically sliced
1    (8-oz.) package dried figs, coarsely chopped (1 cup)
1    Tbsp. balsamic vinegar
Garnish: fresh thyme

1. Combine pomegranate juice, sugar, and ¾ cup water in a
saucepan. Bring to a boil over high heat. Boil 12 to 15 minutes
or until syrupy. Set aside.

2. Meanwhile, combine garlic, thyme, and pepper; rub over
veal. Heat oil in a large skillet over medium-high heat. Brown
veal 2 minutes on each side.

3. Arrange veal in a lightly greased 6-qt. oval slow cooker.
Add shallots to skillet; toss gently. Spoon shallots and figs
over veal. Pour reserved pomegranate syrup over figs. Drizzle
with vinegar. Cover and cook on LOW 6 hours or until tender.
Garnish, if desired.

**Serving Secret: Enjoy this slow-cooked Latin American dish atop black beans and rice inside flour tortillas. Serve with lime wedges.**

# Sweet 'n' Spicy Braised Pork Tacos

hands-on time: 7 min. • total time: 10 hr., 7 min.
makes 8 to 10 servings

3  lb. boneless pork shoulder roast (Boston butt)

½  tsp. salt

½  tsp. freshly ground pepper

1  Tbsp. vegetable oil

2  (14½-oz.) cans diced tomatoes with garlic and onion

1  medium-size sweet onion, chopped

1  to 2 chipotle peppers in adobo sauce, chopped

2  Tbsp. cider vinegar

2  Tbsp. dark brown sugar

¼  tsp. ground cumin

6  cups cooked white rice

1  (15-oz.) can black beans

16 to 20 (6-inch) fajita-size flour tortillas, warmed

Garnishes: fresh cilantro sprigs, lime wedges

**1.** Sprinkle pork with salt and pepper. Cook pork in hot oil in a large skillet over medium-high heat 2 to 3 minutes on all sides or until pork is browned. Stir together tomatoes and next 5 ingredients in a 5-qt. slow cooker. Add pork, turning to coat.

**2.** Cover and cook on LOW 10 hours or until pork is fork-tender. Transfer pork to a cutting board, and let stand 10 minutes. Shred pork with 2 forks. Return shredded pork to slow cooker, and stir until blended. Season with salt and pepper to taste, if desired. Serve immediately with a slotted spoon over rice and black beans in tortillas. Garnish, if desired.

*ideal slow cooker:*
5-quart

*menu idea*
for 8 to 10

Sweet 'n' Spicy Braised Pork Tacos

Strawberries in yogurt

*groceries needed...*

Check staples: salt, pepper, vegetable oil, cider vinegar, dark brown sugar, ground cumin

- 3 lb. boneless pork shoulder roast (Boston butt)
- 2 (14½-oz.) cans diced tomatoes with garlic and onion
- 1 medium-size sweet onion
- 1 (7-oz.) can chipotle peppers in adobo sauce
- 1 (32-oz.) box converted white rice
- 1 (15-oz.) can black beans
- 16 to 20 (6-inch) fajita-size flour tortillas
- 1 bunch cilantro (optional)
- 2 or 3 limes (optional)

*sides...*

- 2 pt. strawberries
- 1 (16-oz.) container vanilla yogurt

*menu idea*

**for 6**

Orange-Molasses
BBQ Ribs

Coleslaw

White bread

Banana pudding

*groceries needed...*

Check staples: cooking spray,
hot sauce (we tested with Tabasco),
jarred minced garlic, salt

- 2 slabs pork baby back ribs (5 lb.)
- 1 (18-oz.) bottle barbecue sauce
  (we tested with Sweet Baby Ray's)
- 1 (12-oz.) jar molasses
- 1 (12-oz.) can frozen orange juice
  concentrate
- 1 orange (optional)

*sides...*

- 1½ pints deli coleslaw
- Loaf of white bread
- 1½ pints deli banana pudding

**Slow-Cooker Secret: Browning the ribs in the oven renders water and excess fat, making the sauce thicker.**

# Orange-Molasses BBQ Ribs

**hands-on time: 11 min. • total time: 8 hr., 22 min.
makes 6 servings**

2  slabs pork baby back ribs (5 lb.), cut in half

1  cup barbecue sauce

¼  cup molasses

¼  cup frozen orange juice concentrate, thawed

2  tsp. hot sauce

1  tsp. jarred minced garlic

¼  tsp. salt

Garnish: orange slices

1. Preheat broiler with oven rack 5½ inches from heat. Coat the rack of a broiler pan and broiler pan with cooking spray. Place ribs on rack in broiler pan. Broil 10 minutes.

2. Meanwhile, stir together barbecue sauce and remaining 5 ingredients in a medium bowl.

3. Arrange ribs in a 6-qt. oval slow cooker. Pour sauce over ribs.

4. Cover and cook on LOW 8 hours. Transfer ribs to a serving platter. Skim fat from juices in slow cooker. Pour juices into a 2-qt. saucepan. Cook over medium-high heat 10 minutes or until reduced to 1½ cups, stirring occasionally. Serve sauce with ribs. Garnish, if desired.

**Ingredient Secret:** Spanish smoked paprika is a popular spice in cooking stores. Known for its deep smoky flavor without the heat, this paprika is a marvelous accent to shrimp dishes, roasted meats, and stews.

*ideal slow cooker:*

5- or 6-quart oval

*menu idea*
### for 6

**Smoked Paprika Pork**

**Long-grain and wild rice**

**Sautéed sugar snap peas**

# Smoked Paprika Pork

hands-on time: 12 min. • total time: 4 hr., 42 min.
makes 6 servings

3     large garlic cloves, pressed
1     tsp. smoked paprika
½     tsp. salt
½     tsp. ground cumin
¼     tsp. freshly ground pepper
1     Tbsp. olive oil
1     (2-lb.) package pork tenderloins
½     cup whipping cream
2     (8.8-oz.) pouches ready-to-serve long-grain and wild rice mix
2     bacon slices, cooked and coarsely crumbled
Chopped fresh chives

**1.** Combine first 5 ingredients. Stir in oil. Pat tenderloins dry with paper towels. Rub paprika paste over tenderloins. Arrange in a greased 5- or 6-qt. oval slow cooker. Cover and cook on HIGH 1 hour. Reduce heat to LOW, and cook 3½ hours or until very tender.

**2.** Remove pork from slow cooker; cover and keep warm on a serving platter. Pour meat drippings into a large skillet. Bring to a boil over medium-high heat. Add whipping cream; boil until slightly thickened, 6 to 7 minutes.

**3.** Meanwhile, microwave rice according to package directions. Spoon rice around pork on platter. Remove sauce from heat; drizzle over pork. Sprinkle with bacon and chives.

*groceries needed...*

Check staples: salt, cumin, pepper, olive oil

* 1 garlic bulb
* 1 (1.62-oz.) jar smoked paprika
* 1 (2-lb.) package pork tenderloins
* 1 pt. whipping cream
* 2 (8.8-oz.) pouches ready-to-serve long-grain and wild rice mix (we tested with Uncle Ben's)
* 1 package bacon
* 1 bunch fresh chives

*side...*
* 1½ lb. sugar snap peas

*menu idea*
**for 6**

Mediterranean
Stuffed Pork
Tenderloin

Orzo

Grilled zucchini

*groceries needed...*

Check staples: salt, pepper, dried Italian
seasoning, cornstarch

* 1 (10-oz.) jar sun-dried tomatoes
  in oil
* 1 jar pitted kalamata olives
* 1 lemon
* 1 garlic bulb
* 2 (1-lb.) pork tenderloins
* 1 (4-oz.) package crumbled feta
  cheese
* 1 (14.5-oz.) can diced tomatoes
  with basil, garlic, and oregano

*sides...*

* 1 (16-oz.) bag orzo
* 1 lb. zucchini

# Mediterranean Stuffed Pork Tenderloin

**hands-on time: 15 min. • total time: 3 hr., 27 min.**
**makes 6 servings**

⅓  cup drained sun-dried tomatoes in oil, chopped

3½  Tbsp. oil from sun-dried tomatoes in oil, divided

1¼  tsp. salt, divided

¾  tsp. pepper, divided

1  Tbsp. dried Italian seasoning

2  Tbsp. chopped pitted kalamata olives

¾  tsp. lemon zest

2  garlic cloves, pressed

2  (1-lb.) pork tenderloins

½  cup (2 oz.) crumbled feta cheese

1  (14.5-oz.) can diced tomatoes with basil, garlic, and oregano, undrained

1  Tbsp. cornstarch

**1.** Place sun-dried tomatoes in a small bowl. Stir in 2 Tbsp. sun-dried tomato oil, 1 tsp. salt, ½ tsp. pepper, and next 4 ingredients. Butterfly pork by making a lengthwise cut down center of 1 side of each tenderloin, cutting to within ½ inch of other side. Unfold, forming 2 rectangles. Sprinkle with ⅛ tsp. salt and ⅛ tsp. pepper. Spread half of sun-dried tomato mixture over each tenderloin, leaving a ½-inch border; sprinkle with cheese. Fold long sides of tenderloins together to enclose filling; secure with wooden picks. Heat remaining 1½ Tbsp. sun-dried tomato oil in a skillet; add stuffed tenderloins. Cook 4 minutes, turning occasionally until browned on all sides. Place tenderloins, seam side up, in a 5-qt. slow cooker; add diced tomatoes. Cover; cook on LOW 3 hours.

**2.** Remove tenderloins to a platter, reserving tomato mixture in slow cooker; cover and let stand 10 to 15 minutes.

**3.** Meanwhile, stir together cornstarch and 2 Tbsp. water until smooth; stir into tomato mixture. Increase heat to HIGH; cook 10 minutes or until slightly thickened. Remove wooden picks; cut tenderloins into slices. Spoon tomato gravy over pork slices.

**Slow-Cooker Secret:** The thickness of the pork chops is essential in this recipe. It ensures that this lean cut of pork stays tender and juicy throughout the long cook time.

*ideal slow cooker:*

5-quart

# Spiced Apple Pork Chops

hands-on time: 12 min. • total time: 6 hr., 12 min.
makes 4 servings

4    (1¼-inch-thick) pork chops (about 3 lb.)
1    tsp. salt, divided
½    tsp. pepper
1    (8-oz.) container refrigerated prechopped onion (about 1¾ cups)
½    cup raisins
2    (5-oz.) packages dried apples
½    cup firmly packed brown sugar
1    Tbsp. ground cinnamon
½    tsp. ground cloves
½    tsp. ground ginger

**1.** Sprinkle pork with ½ tsp. salt and pepper. Heat a large nonstick skillet over medium-high heat. Add pork to pan; cook 3 minutes on each side or until browned. Transfer pork to a lightly greased 5-qt. slow cooker, reserving drippings in pan.

**2.** Sauté onion in drippings 3 minutes or until tender. Add onion, remaining ½ tsp. salt, 2 cups water, raisins, and remaining 5 ingredients to pork in slow cooker. Cover and cook on LOW 6 hours.

*menu idea*
for 4

**Spiced Apple Pork Chops**

**Mashed sweet potatoes**

**Sautéed Brussels sprouts**

**Apple cider**

*groceries needed...*

Check staples: salt, pepper, brown sugar, cinnamon, cloves, ginger

- 4 (1¼-inch-thick) pork chops (about 3 lb.)
- 1 (8-oz.) container refrigerated prechopped onion
- 1 (12-oz.) package raisins
- 2 (5-oz.) packages dried apples

*sides...*

- 1 (24-oz.) package frozen mashed sweet potatoes
- 1 lb. fresh Brussels sprouts
- 1 container apple cider

*menu idea*

**for 6**

**Pimiento Cheese Grits With Ham**

**Green beans**

**Biscuits**

*groceries needed...*

Check staples: butter, pepper

* 1 (32-oz.) container plus 1 (14-oz.) can low-sodium fat-free chicken broth
* 1 lb. uncooked stone-ground yellow grits
* 1 lb. smoked fully cooked ham
* 3 (2-oz.) jars diced pimiento
* 1 (8-oz.) package shredded Cheddar cheese
* 1 (8-oz.) package shredded Swiss cheese
* 1 pt. heavy cream

*sides...*

* 1½ lb. fresh green beans
* 1 package frozen biscuits

**Flavor Secret: Add a little heat to the entrée by stirring in some chopped jalapeño peppers.**

# Pimiento Cheese Grits With Ham

hands-on time: 4 min. • total time: 6 hr., 4 min.
makes 6 servings

4½ cups low-sodium fat-free chicken broth

3 Tbsp. butter, melted

1½ cups uncooked stone-ground yellow grits

½ tsp. freshly ground pepper

1 lb. smoked fully cooked ham, cut into 1-inch cubes

3 (2-oz.) jars diced pimiento, drained

1 cup (4 oz.) shredded Cheddar cheese

½ cup (2 oz.) shredded Swiss cheese

½ cup heavy cream

**1.** Whisk together broth and butter in a lightly greased 4-qt. slow cooker; gradually whisk in grits and pepper. Stir in ham and pimiento. Cover and cook on LOW 6 hours, stirring after 3 hours.

**2.** Stir in cheeses and cream. Serve immediately.

**Substitution Secret:** This family-friendly pasta dish is adaptable. Use your favorite type of frozen peas, and substitute whipping cream and Gruyère cheese for easy alternatives to the half-and-half and Swiss cheese.

# Cheesy Ham and Noodles

hands-on time: 9 min. • total time: 3 hr., 9 min.
makes 6 servings

12  oz. uncooked linguine
3   cups half-and-half
2   cups (8 oz.) shredded Swiss cheese
1   cup frozen peas
1   Tbsp. Dijon mustard
1   (12-oz.) lean ham steak, chopped
1   (10-oz.) package refrigerated Alfredo sauce

1. Bring water to a boil in a 4-qt. saucepan. Cook linguine 5 minutes; drain. Transfer pasta to a lightly greased 4-qt. slow cooker. Add half-and-half, 1 cup cheese, and remaining 4 ingredients, stirring gently to blend. Sprinkle with remaining 1 cup cheese. Cover and cook on LOW 3 hours or until pasta is tender.

*ideal slow cooker:*
4-quart

*menu idea*
for 6

Cheesy Ham
and Noodles

Steamed broccoli

Rolls

*groceries needed...*
Check staples: Dijon mustard
❋ 1 (16-oz.) package linguine
❋ 1 qt. half-and-half
❋ 1 (8-oz.) package shredded Swiss cheese
❋ 1 (10-oz.) package frozen peas
❋ 1 (12-oz.) lean ham steak
❋ 1 (10-oz.) package refrigerated Alfredo sauce

*sides...*
❋ 1 bunch broccoli
❋ Rolls

*menu idea*

### for 8

**Sausage, Red Beans, and Rice**

**Cornbread**

*groceries needed...*

Check staples: salt, oregano, dried thyme, ground red pepper, hot sauce

❋ 1 (16-oz.) package dried red beans

❋ 1 lb. smoked sausage

❋ 1 onion

❋ 1 bunch fresh parsley

❋ 1 garlic bulb

❋ 2 (8.8-oz.) packages microwaveable long-grain rice

❋ 1 bunch green onions

*side...*

❋ Favorite cornbread

**Serving Secret: This homey recipe will please a crowd on game day just as easily as it will make a hearty family meal any day.**

# Sausage, Red Beans, and Rice

hands-on time: 14 min. • total time: 16 hr., 14 min.
makes 8 servings

| | |
|---|---|
| 1 | (16-oz.) package dried red beans |
| 1 | lb. smoked sausage, sliced |
| 1 | cup chopped onion |
| ¾ | cup chopped parsley |
| 1 | tsp. salt |
| ½ | tsp. dried oregano |
| ½ | tsp. dried thyme |
| ⅛ | tsp. ground red pepper |
| 3 | garlic cloves, minced |

Hot cooked rice

Hot sauce

Chopped green onions

**1.** Rinse and sort beans according to package directions. Cover with water 2 inches above beans; let soak 8 hours. Drain and place in a 5-qt. slow cooker.

**2.** Sauté sausage and onion in a large skillet over medium-high heat 5 minutes or until sausage is browned and onion is tender.

**3.** Stir sausage mixture, 5 cups water, parsley, and next 5 ingredients into beans. Cover and cook on LOW 8 hours. Mash beans with a potato masher or the back of a spoon to desired consistency. Serve with hot cooked rice and hot sauce; sprinkle with green onions.

# Louisiana-Style Smothered Pork Chops

hands-on time: 15 min. • total time: 6 hr., 25 min.
makes 4 servings

4   oz. smoked sausage, chopped

3   Tbsp. all-purpose flour

1   tsp. salt

½   tsp. pepper

4   (1¼-inch-thick) bone-in center-cut pork chops

3   Tbsp. vegetable oil

1   (16-oz.) package gumbo frozen vegetable mix

1   (14-oz.) can chicken broth

½   tsp. dried thyme

1   Tbsp. cornstarch

Hot cooked rice

4   green onions, sliced

Hot sauce (optional)

**1.** Sauté sausage in a large skillet over medium-high heat until browned. Drain sausage, reserving drippings in pan.

**2.** Combine flour, salt, and pepper in a large zip-top plastic freezer bag; add pork chops. Seal bag, and shake to coat.

**3.** Add oil to drippings in skillet. Cook pork chops in hot oil over medium-high heat 3 minutes on each side or until browned. Transfer pork chops to a 5- to 6-qt. slow cooker. Layer vegetables and sausage over pork chops; add broth and thyme. Cover and cook on LOW 6 hours.

**4.** Remove pork chops from slow cooker; cover and keep warm. Increase temperature to HIGH. Combine cornstarch and 2 tablespoons water, stirring until smooth. Stir cornstarch mixture into vegetables in slow cooker. Cook, uncovered, 10 more minutes or until thickened.

**5.** Spoon rice onto serving plates; top with pork chops. Spoon vegetables and sauce over pork chops. Sprinkle vegetables with green onions, and serve with hot sauce, if desired.

*ideal slow cooker:*

5- or 6-quart

*menu idea*
**for 4**

Louisiana-Style
Smothered
Pork Chops

French bread

*groceries needed...*

Check staples: flour, salt, pepper, vegetable oil, dried thyme, cornstarch, hot sauce (optional)

- 1 package smoked sausage
- 4 (1¼-inch-thick) bone-in center-cut pork chops
- 1 (16-oz.) package gumbo frozen vegetable mix
- 1 (14-oz.) can chicken broth
- 2 (8.8-oz.) packages microwaveable long-grain rice
- 1 bunch green onions

*side...*
- 1 loaf French bread

*menu idea*

**for 6**

Mushroom-and-
Sausage Wild Rice
With Pecans
and Raisins

Sautéed spinach

*groceries needed...*

Check staples: kosher salt, pepper

• 1 lb. ground pork sausage
• 1 (8-oz.) container refrigerated prechopped onion
• 1 (8-oz.) package sliced fresh mushrooms
• 1 box wild rice
• 1 (32-oz.) container chicken broth
• 1 box converted long-grain rice
• 1 (12-oz.) package raisins
• 1 bunch fresh thyme
• 1 container chopped pecans

*side...*

• 2 (10-oz.) packages chopped spinach

Slow-Cooker Secret: Converted rice is the secret to fluffy, tender rice in the slow cooker. We find that it holds its shape better during prolonged cooking than regular long-grain rice.

# Mushroom-and-Sausage Wild Rice With Pecans and Raisins

hands-on time: 15 min. • total time: 2 hr., 45 min.
makes 6 servings

1   lb. ground pork sausage
1   (8-oz.) container refrigerated prechopped onion
1   (8-oz.) package sliced fresh mushrooms
⅓   cup wild rice
3   cups chicken broth
2   cups converted long-grain rice
⅔   cup raisins
1½  tsp. chopped fresh thyme
½   tsp. kosher salt
½   tsp. freshly ground pepper
½   cup coarsely chopped pecans, toasted

1. Brown sausage in a large skillet over medium-high heat, stirring often, 5 minutes or until meat crumbles and is no longer pink; drain, reserving 2 tablespoons drippings in pan. Sauté onion, mushrooms, and wild rice in hot drippings 5 minutes or until vegetables are tender. Add broth to vegetables, stirring to loosen particles from bottom of skillet.

2. Place sausage, rice, and next 4 ingredients in a lightly greased 5-qt. slow cooker; stir in broth mixture. Cover and cook on LOW 2½ hours or until liquid is absorbed and rice is tender. Add pecans to rice; fluff with a fork.

**Ingredient Secret:** Open sausage casings using kitchen shears; then just squeeze the sausage into the pan for browning.

# Baked Four-Cheese Spaghetti With Italian Sausage

hands-on time: 15 min. • total time: 3 hr., 25 min.
makes 8 to 10 servings

| | |
|---|---|
| 8 | oz. uncooked spaghetti |
| 1 | lb. Italian sausage (about 4 links) |
| 1 | (8-oz.) container refrigerated prechopped bell pepper-and-onion mix |
| 2 | tsp. jarred minced garlic |
| 1 | Tbsp. vegetable oil |
| 1 | (24-oz.) jar fire-roasted tomato and garlic pasta sauce |
| 1 | (16-oz.) package shredded sharp Cheddar cheese |
| 1 | (8-oz.) package shredded mozzarella cheese, divided |
| 4 | oz. fontina cheese, shredded |
| ½ | cup (2 oz.) preshredded Parmesan cheese |

1. Cook pasta in boiling salted water in a large Dutch oven according to package directions. Drain and return to pan.

2. Meanwhile, brown sausage, bell pepper mix, and garlic in oil in a large nonstick skillet over medium-high heat, stirring often, 8 to 10 minutes or until meat crumbles and is no longer pink. Drain. Stir meat mixture, pasta sauce, and Cheddar cheese into pasta. Spoon half of pasta mixture into a lightly greased 5-qt. slow cooker coated with cooking spray.

3. Combine mozzarella cheese and fontina cheese. Sprinkle half of mozzarella mixture over pasta mixture in slow cooker. Top with remaining pasta mixture, remaining mozzarella mixture, and Parmesan cheese. Cover and cook on LOW 3 hours. Let stand, covered, 10 minutes before serving.

*groceries needed...*

Check staples: jarred minced garlic, vegetable oil, cooking spray, salad dressing

- 1 (16-oz.) package spaghetti
- 1 lb. Italian sausage (about 4 links)
- 1 (8-oz.) container refrigerated prechopped bell pepper-and-onion mix
- 1 (24-oz.) jar fire-roasted tomato and garlic pasta sauce (we tested with Classico)
- 1 (16-oz.) package shredded sharp Cheddar cheese
- 1 (8-oz.) package shredded mozzarella cheese
- 4 oz. fontina cheese
- 1 container preshredded Parmesan cheese

*side...*

- 2 (5-oz.) packages mixed salad greens

# {quick-fix breads}

### Herbed Goat Cheese Toasts

Combine ½ cup crumbled goat cheese, ¾ tsp. dried oregano, ½ tsp. garlic powder, ¼ tsp. paprika, and ⅛ tsp. salt; sprinkle over 8 (1-oz) slices French bread. Broil for 2 minutes or until lightly browned.

### Crusty Italian Bread With Herbed Olive Oil

In a small skillet, heat ¼ cup olive oil; add 1 tsp. dried Italian seasoning and 1 tsp. minced garlic. Sauté 2 minutes. Serve with Italian bread.

### Oregano Breadsticks

Preheat oven to 375°. Brush prefrigerated breadstick dough with 1 Tbsp. olive oil; sprinkle with 1 tsp. dried oregano. Separate dough into individual breadsticks. Place dough sticks on a baking sheet coated with cooking spray. Bake at 375° for 13 minutes or until lightly browned.

# poultry pleasers

A slow cooker simmering away means that at the end of the day a hearty meal awaits your family with practically no effort at all. Today's poultry makes a great dinner choice because it's rich in nutrients, low in fat, reasonably priced, and abundant. These trusty recipes offer options for using chicken breasts, whole cooked chicken, or turkey. Prized for its tender white meat and moist dark meat, poultry prepared in a slow cooker is a surefire winner.

**Ingredient Secret: Preshredded carrots speed up the preparation time.**

# Slow-Cooker Chicken Paprikash

hands-on time: 12 min. • total time: 7 hr., 12 min.
makes 6 servings

3   Tbsp. all-purpose flour
2   lb. skinned and boned chicken breasts, cut into ½-inch strips
2   cups chopped onion
1¼  cups low-sodium fat-free chicken broth
1   cup chopped red bell pepper
½   cup shredded carrot
2   Tbsp. Hungarian sweet paprika
2   tsp. jarred minced garlic
1   tsp. salt
1   tsp. freshly ground black pepper
1   (8-oz.) package sliced mushrooms
1¼  cups sour cream

1. Combine flour and chicken in a medium bowl; toss well. Add chicken mixture, chopped onion, and next 8 ingredients to a 4-qt. slow cooker. Cover and cook on HIGH for 1 hour; turn to LOW, and cook 6 hours. Stir in sour cream.

*ideal slow cooker:*

4-quart

*menu idea*
**for 6**

Slow-Cooker
Chicken Paprikash

Orzo

*groceries needed...*

Check staples: flour, jarred minced garlic, salt, pepper

* 2 lb. skinned and boned chicken breasts
* 1 large onion
* 1 (14-oz.) can low-sodium fat-free chicken broth
* 1 red bell pepper
* 1 bundle carrots
* Hungarian sweet paprika
* 1 (8-oz.) package sliced mushrooms
* 1 (8-oz.) container sour cream

*side...*

* 1 (16-oz.) package orzo

*groceries needed...*

- 2 (10-oz.) cans mild green chile enchilada sauce (we tested with Old El Paso)
- 10 (6-inch) corn tortillas
- 4 (4-oz.) skinned and boned chicken breasts
- 1 (16-oz.) container sour cream
- 1 (12-oz.) package shredded colby-Jack cheese blend
- 1 (10¾-oz.) can cream of mushroom soup
- 1 head iceberg lettuce
- 1 (15-oz.) can black beans
- 3 tomatoes

*sides...*

- 1 large bag tortilla chips
- 1 jar salsa
- 3 or 4 tomatoes

**Slow-Cooker Secret: The corn tortillas cook into this dish and thicken it—you won't see them after they're cooked, but you will still taste their authentic Mexican flavor.**

# Chicken Enchilada Dip

**hands-on time: 10 min.** • **total time: 4 hr., 10 min.**
**makes 8 servings**

| | |
|---|---|
| 2 | (10-oz.) cans mild green chile enchilada sauce |
| 10 | (6-inch) corn tortillas, torn into 3-inch pieces |
| 4 | cups pulled cooked chicken breasts |
| 1½ | cups sour cream |
| 1 | (12-oz.) package shredded colby-Jack cheese blend, divided |
| 1 | (10¾-oz.) can cream of mushroom soup |
| 8 | cups shredded iceberg lettuce |
| 1 | (15-oz.) can black beans |
| 3 | tomatoes, diced |

**1.** Spoon ½ cup enchilada sauce over bottom of a greased 4-qt. slow cooker. Add enough tortilla pieces to cover sauce.

**2.** Stir together chicken, sour cream, 2 cups cheese, and soup. Spread 2 cups chicken mixture over tortilla pieces. Top with tortilla pieces to cover. Drizzle with ½ cup enchilada sauce. Repeat layers twice, ending with tortilla pieces, and remaining enchilada sauce. Sprinkle with remaining 1 cup cheese.

**3.** Cover and cook on LOW 4 hours. Place lettuce on plates; top with chicken, beans, and tomatoes. Serve hot.

# Chicken and Dumplings

hands-on time: 15 min. • total time: 8 hr., 38 min.
makes 8 servings

5    large carrots, cut into 2-inch pieces

3    small Yukon gold potatoes, unpeeled and cut into chunks

6    skinned and boned chicken breasts

1    tsp. salt

1    tsp. freshly ground pepper

1    cup chicken broth or water

2    (10¾-oz.) cans cream of chicken soup

Freshly ground pepper

1    cup frozen peas

2    hard-cooked eggs, chopped

2    cups all-purpose baking mix

⅔    cup half-and-half or milk

2    Tbsp. chopped fresh herbs such as flat-leaf parsley, thyme, and rosemary

Garnishes: chopped fresh herbs, freshly ground pepper

1. Place carrot and potato in a lightly greased 6-qt. slow cooker.

2. Sprinkle chicken with 1 tsp. each of salt and pepper. Heat a large nonstick skillet over medium-high heat. Coat with cooking spray. Sauté chicken, in 2 batches, 2 minutes on each side or until browned. Place chicken over vegetables in slow cooker. Stir together broth and soup; pour over chicken. Sprinkle with freshly ground pepper.

3. Cover and cook on LOW 7 hours. Add peas and egg, stirring gently to break up chicken into bite-size pieces.

4. Combine baking mix, half-and-half, and herbs; stir with a fork until blended. Drop by 8 spoonfuls onto chicken mixture. Cover and cook on HIGH 1 hour and 15 minutes or until dumplings are done. Garnish, if desired.

*ideal slow cooker:*
6-quart

*menu idea*
for 8

Chicken and
Dumplings
Deli Waldorf salad

*groceries needed...*

Check staples: salt, pepper, eggs, all-purpose baking mix, half-and-half or milk

* 5 large carrots
* 3 small Yukon gold potatoes
* 6 skinned and boned chicken breasts
* 1 (14-oz.) can chicken broth
* 2 (10¾-oz.) cans cream of chicken soup
* 1 (10-oz.) package frozen peas
* 1 bunch fresh herbs (flat-leaf parsley, thyme, and rosemary) (optional)

*side...*

* 1 qt. deli Waldorf salad

*groceries needed...*

Check staples: milk, butter

- 6 skinned and boned chicken breasts
- 2 (10¾-oz.) cans cream of chicken soup
- Poppy seeds
- 1 box round buttery crackers

*sides...*

- 2 (8.8-oz.) packages quick-cooking wild rice mix
- 1 bunch broccoli

**Slow-Cooker Secret: Don't be tempted to sprinkle on the crumb mixture while chicken is in the cooker—condensation will cause breadcrumbs to become soggy.**

# Poppy-Seed Chicken

hands-on time: 5 min. • total time: 4 hr., 5 min.
makes 6 servings

| | |
|---|---|
| 6 | skinned and boned chicken breasts |
| 2 | (10¾-oz.) cans cream of chicken soup |
| 1 | cup milk |
| 1 | Tbsp. poppy seeds |
| 36 | round buttery crackers, crushed |
| ¼ | cup butter, melted |

1. Place chicken in a lightly greased 6-qt. oval slow cooker. Whisk together soup, milk, and poppy seeds in a medium bowl; pour over chicken. Cover and cook on HIGH 1 hour.

2. Reduce heat to LOW, and cook 3 hours.

3. Combine cracker crumbs and butter, stirring until crumbs are moistened. Sprinkle over chicken just before serving.

**Shopping Secret: Shop for the "value-size" jar of pasta sauce. It's the ideal amount for this recipe, especially if chicken breasts are on the large size. Otherwise, pick up 2 (24-oz.) jars and enjoy about ½ cup leftover sauce on a small pizza.**

*ideal slow cooker:*
6- or 7-quart oval

*menu idea*
for 6

Chicken Parmesan
Spaghetti
Mixed green salad
Grissini

# Chicken Parmesan

hands-on time: 12 min. • total time: 3 hr., 47 min.
makes 6 servings

| | |
|---|---|
| 2 | cups Italian-seasoned Japanese breadcrumbs (panko) |
| 6 | skinned and boned chicken breasts |
| 2 | large eggs, lightly beaten |
| 4 | Tbsp. olive oil, divided |
| 1 | (44-oz.) jar tomato-basil sauce |
| ¾ | tsp. salt |
| ½ | tsp. pepper |
| 1 | (8-oz.) package shredded mozzarella cheese |
| ¾ | cup (3 oz.) shredded Parmesan cheese |

Garnish: fresh oregano

**1.** Spread breadcrumbs on a large plate. Dip chicken in beaten egg, 1 breast at a time. Dredge chicken in breadcrumbs, pressing gently for crumbs to adhere.

**2.** Heat 2 Tbsp. oil in a large nonstick skillet over medium-high heat. Cook chicken, in 2 batches, 2 minutes on each side or until browned, adding remaining 2 Tbsp. oil with second batch.

**3.** Pour sauce into a lightly greased 6- or 7-qt. oval slow cooker. Arrange chicken in slow cooker over sauce. Sprinkle with salt and pepper. Cover and cook on HIGH 3½ hours. Add cheeses; cover and cook on HIGH 5 more minutes or until cheese melts. Garnish, if desired.

*groceries needed...*

Check staples: eggs, olive oil, salt, pepper, salad dressing

* 1 (8-oz.) box Italian-seasoned Japanese breadcrumbs (panko)
* 6 skinned and boned chicken breasts
* 1 (44-oz.) jar tomato-basil sauce (we tested with Classico)
* 1 (8-oz.) package shredded mozzarella cheese
* ¾ cup (3 oz.) shredded Parmesan cheese
* 1 bunch fresh oregano (optional)

*sides...*

* 1 (16-oz.) package spaghetti
* Grissini
* Mixed salad greens

*ideal slow cooker:*

**5-quart**

*menu idea*
**for 6**

Slow-Cooker
Chicken Tostados

Chocolate chip
cookies

*groceries needed...*

Check staples: flour

* 1 (14-oz.) can chicken broth
* 1 jar salsa
* 1 large onion
* 2½ lb. skinned and boned chicken breasts
* 1 (8-oz.) container sour cream
* 6 (8-inch) flour tortillas
* 1 (8-oz.) bag shredded lettuce
* 1 (15-oz.) can red beans
* 2 cups (8 oz.) shredded sharp Cheddar cheese
* 1 large tomato

*side...*

* 1 package chocolate chip cookies

**Flavor Secret: You can serve all kinds of toppings such as sour cream, salsa, chopped avocado, or cilantro with this delicious dish.**

# Slow-Cooker Chicken Tostados

hands-on time: 12 min. · total time: 7 hr., 12 min.
makes 6 servings

| | |
|---|---|
| ¾ | cup chicken broth |
| ½ | cup salsa |
| ⅓ | cup all-purpose flour |
| 1 | large onion, chopped |
| 2½ | lb. skinned and boned chicken breasts |
| ⅔ | cup sour cream |

**Vegetable oil**

| | |
|---|---|
| 6 | (8-inch) flour tortillas |
| 1 | (8-oz.) bag shredded lettuce |
| 1 | (15-oz.) can red beans, heated |
| 2 | cups (8 oz.) shredded sharp Cheddar cheese |
| 1 | large tomato, chopped |

1. Combine broth, salsa, and flour in a 5-qt. slow cooker, whisking to blend. Stir in onion. Arrange chicken in slow cooker, smooth side up. Cover and cook on HIGH for 1 hour; reduce heat to LOW, and cook for 6 hours. Shred chicken, and stir in sour cream.

2. Return chicken mixture to slow cooker. Keep warm until ready to serve.

3. Pour oil to a depth of ¼ inch into a heavy skillet. Fry tortillas, 1 at a time, in hot oil over high heat 20 seconds on each side or until crisp and golden brown. Drain on paper towels.

4. Layer lettuce, beans, chicken mixture, cheese, and chopped tomato on warm tortillas.

**Slow-Cooker Secret:** All the flavor of traditional sesame chicken is in this recipe, but without the work of breading and frying the chicken pieces.

# Sesame Chicken

hands-on time: 7 min. • total time: 2 hr., 37 min.
makes 4 to 6 servings

1¼ cups chicken broth

½ cup firmly packed brown sugar

¼ cup cornstarch

2 Tbsp. rice vinegar

2 Tbsp. soy sauce

2 Tbsp. sweet chili sauce

2 Tbsp. honey

2 tsp. dark sesame oil

1½ lb. skinned and boned chicken breasts, cut into 1-inch pieces

2 cups sugar snap peas

2 cups crinkle-cut carrots

1½ Tbsp. sesame seeds, toasted

Hot cooked rice

Garnish: chopped green onions

1. Whisk together first 8 ingredients in a 4-qt. slow cooker. Stir in chicken. Cover and cook on HIGH 2½ hours or until chicken is done, stirring after 1½ hours.

2. Steam sugar snap peas and carrots. Stir vegetable mixture and sesame seeds into slow cooker. Serve over hot cooked rice. Garnish, if desired.

*menu idea*
for 4 to 6

**Sesame Chicken**

**Hot cooked rice**

*groceries needed...*

Check staples: brown sugar, cornstarch, rice vinegar, soy sauce, honey

* 1 lb. bag sugar snap peas
* 1 (16-oz.) package crinkle-cut carrots
* 1 (14-oz.) can chicken broth
* 1 (12-oz.) bottle sweet chili sauce
* 1 bottle dark sesame oil
* 1½ lb. skinned and boned chicken breasts
* Sesame seeds
* 1 bunch green onions

*side...*

* 1 (14-oz.) package boil-in-bag rice

*menu idea*
**for 8**

Chicken, Broccoli,
Bacon, and Rice

Orange sections

Dinner rolls

*groceries needed...*

Check staples: salt, pepper

- 1 package slow cooker liners
- 1 (14-oz) package instant rice
- 6 skinned and boned chicken breasts
- 1 small package matchsticks carrots
- 1 (8-oz.) package shredded sharp Cheddar cheese
- 1 (8-oz.) package frozen prechopped onion
- 1 (8-oz.) can sliced water chestnuts
- 2 (10¼-oz.) cans cream of chicken soup
- 1 (12-oz.) package bacon
- 1 (16-oz.) package frozen broccoli cuts
- 1 package ridged potato chips

*sides...*

- 8 oranges
- 1 package dinner rolls

**Slow-Cooker Secret: Chicken easily breaks apart after 5 or more hours of slow cooking on LOW. Stir gently, cutting up chicken with a spoon as you stir.**

# Chicken, Broccoli, Bacon, and Rice

hands-on time: 8 min. · total time: 7 hr., 16 min.
makes 8 servings

| | |
|---|---|
| 1 | slow cooker liner |
| 1½ | cups instant white rice |
| 6 | skinned and boned chicken breasts |
| 1 | tsp. salt |
| ½ | tsp. pepper |
| 1 | cup matchstick carrots |
| 2 | cups (8 oz.) shredded sharp Cheddar cheese |
| 1 | cup frozen prechopped onion |
| 1 | (8-oz.) can sliced water chestnuts, drained |
| 2 | (10¾-oz.) cans cream of chicken soup |
| 6 | fully cooked bacon slices |
| 1 | (16-oz.) package frozen broccoli cuts (do not thaw) |
| 2 | to 3 cups coarsely crushed ridged potato chips |

**1.** Place slow cooker liner in a 5- or 6-qt. slow cooker. Coat liner with cooking spray. Place rice in liner. Sprinkle chicken with salt and pepper. Heat a large nonstick skillet over medium-high heat. Coat pan with cooking spray. Sauté chicken, in 2 batches, 2 minutes on each side or until browned. Place on top of rice. Top with carrots, 1 cup cheese, onion, and water chestnuts. Sprinkle with remaining 1 cup cheese. Top with soup. Pour 1½ cups water around edges.

**2.** Cover and cook on LOW 6 hours, stirring gently after 5 hours to break up chicken into chunks. Coarsely crumble bacon; add to slow cooker. Stir in broccoli. Cover and cook on LOW 1 more hour. Top with chips before serving.

# Creamy Mustard Chicken With Leeks

hands-on time: 5 min. • total time: 3 hr., 13 min.
makes 6 servings

2    medium leeks, sliced
2    Tbsp. olive oil
6    skinned and boned chicken breasts
¾    tsp. salt, divided
¾    tsp. freshly ground pepper, divided
¼    cup whipping cream
3    Tbsp. coarse-grained mustard
5    garlic cloves, minced
1    (10¾-oz.) can cream of chicken soup

**Hot cooked rice**

**1.** Place leeks in a lightly greased 5-qt. slow cooker.

**2.** Heat oil in a large nonstick skillet over medium-high heat. Sprinkle chicken with ½ tsp. each salt and pepper. Sauté chicken, in 2 batches, 2 minutes on each side or until browned. Place chicken in slow cooker.

**3.** Combine remaining ¼ tsp. each of salt and pepper, whipping cream, and next 3 ingredients; pour over chicken in slow cooker. Cover and cook on LOW 3 hours. Serve over hot cooked rice.

*ideal slow cooker:*
5-quart

*menu idea*
for 6

**Creamy Mustard Chicken With Leeks**

**Hot cooked rice**

**Asparagus**

**Green salad with mandarin oranges and strawberries**

*groceries needed...*

Check staples: olive oil, salt, pepper, salad dressing

* 2 medium leeks
* 6 skinned and boned chicken breasts
* ½ pint whipping cream
* 1 small bottle coarse-grained mustard
* 1 garlic bulb
* 1 (10¾-oz.) can cream of chicken soup

*sides...*

* 1 (14-oz.) package boil-in-bag rice
* 1 bundle asparagus
* 1 (8-oz.) package mixed salad greens
* 1 (11-oz.) can mandarin oranges
* 1 pt. strawberries

*menu idea*
for 6

**Chicken With Wine-Mushroom Gravy**

**Brown rice**

**Roasted carrots**

*groceries needed...*

Check staples: salt, pepper, olive oil

* 6 skinned and boned chicken breasts
* 1 (8-oz.) package sliced fresh mushrooms
* 1 large shallot
* 1 bottle dry white wine
* 1 (10¾-oz.) can cream of mushroom soup
* 1 (16-oz.) container sour cream
* 1 bunch fresh parsley

*sides...*

* 1 (14-oz.) package boil-in-bag brown rice
* 1 (2-lb.) bag carrots

**Flavor Secret: Searing chicken breasts briefly in a hot skillet gets a jump start on cooking and developing rich flavor.**

# Chicken With Wine-Mushroom Gravy

hands-on time: 15 min.  •  total time: 3 hr., 15 min.
makes 6 servings

| | |
|---|---|
| 6 | skinned and boned chicken breasts |
| ¼ | tsp. salt |
| ¼ | tsp. pepper |
| 1 | Tbsp. olive oil |
| 1 | (8-oz.) package sliced fresh mushrooms |
| 1 | large shallot, minced |
| 1 | cup dry white wine |
| 1 | (10¾-oz.) can cream of mushroom soup |
| 2 | cups sour cream |
| 2 | Tbsp. chopped fresh parsley |

**1.** Sprinkle chicken with salt and pepper. Heat oil in a large skillet over medium-high heat. Add chicken to skillet; cook 3 minutes on each side or until browned. Place chicken in a lightly greased 5-qt. slow cooker.

**2.** Add mushrooms to skillet; sauté on high heat 4 minutes or until browned. Add shallot; cook 1 more minute. Whisk in wine and soup until blended. Pour mushroom mixture over chicken.

**3.** Cover and cook on LOW 3 hours or until chicken is done. Remove chicken to a serving platter. Stir sour cream into juices in slow cooker; spoon over chicken. Sprinkle with parsley.

groceries needed...

Check staples: salt, pepper, olive oil

- 4 skinned and boned chicken breasts
- 1 (14-oz.) bottle buffalo wing sauce (we tested with Budweiser Wing Sauce)
- 1 package celery ribs
- 1 package matchstick carrots
- 1 red onion
- 1 bottle blue cheese dressing
- 1 package bakery-style buns or kaiser rolls

side...

- Green grapes

Flavor Secret: The flavor of restaurant-style wings develops in the slow cooker; then the chicken is shredded and piled onto sandwiches. A quick-toss carrot slaw tames the heat.

# Buffalo Chicken Sandwiches

hands-on time: 7 min. • total time: 3 hr., 9 min.
makes 6 servings

| | |
|---|---|
| 4 | skinned and boned chicken breasts |
| 1/4 | tsp. salt |
| 1/8 | tsp. freshly ground pepper |
| 1 | Tbsp. olive oil |
| 1 | (14-oz.) bottle buffalo wing sauce, divided |
| 2 | small celery ribs |
| 3/4 | cup matchstick carrots |
| 1 | Tbsp. thinly sliced red onion |
| 1/3 | cup refrigerated blue cheese dressing |
| 6 | bakery-style buns or kaiser rolls, lightly toasted |

1. Sprinkle chicken with salt and ground red pepper. Heat oil in a large nonstick skillet over medium-high heat. Add chicken; cook 2 minutes on each side or until lightly browned. Transfer chicken to a 4-qt. slow cooker. Reserve 2 Tbsp. wing sauce. Pour remaining wing sauce over chicken. Cover and cook on LOW 3 hours or until chicken is done.

2. Meanwhile, thinly slice celery crosswise to measure 3/4 cup. Combine reserved 2 Tbsp. wing sauce, celery, carrot, and next 2 ingredients; toss to coat.

3. Shred chicken in a bowl with 2 forks; toss with 1/2 cup cooking liquid from slow cooker. Serve shredded chicken on buns; top with carrot slaw.

# Chicken Chow Mein

hands-on time: 10 min. • total time: 3 hr., 10 min.
makes 6 to 8 servings

1   red bell pepper, cut into strips
2   lb. chicken breast tenders or 2 lb. skinned and boned
    chicken breasts, cut into strips
½   tsp. pepper
1   Tbsp. vegetable oil
½   cup lite soy sauce
¼   cup oyster sauce
1   Tbsp. dark sesame oil
2   tsp. grated fresh ginger
1   Tbsp. cornstarch
2   cups frozen broccoli cuts (do not thaw)
1   cup shelled frozen edamame (green soybeans) (do not thaw)
2   (8-oz.) cans sliced water chestnuts, drained
3   green onions, diagonally sliced
Hot cooked rice
½   cup cashews (optional)
1   (3-oz.) can chow mein noodles (optional)

**1.** Place bell pepper strips in a lightly greased 4- or 5-qt. slow cooker. Sprinkle chicken with pepper. Heat oil in a large non-stick skillet over medium-high heat. Sauté chicken 2 minutes on each side; transfer to slow cooker.

**2.** Combine soy sauce and next 3 ingredients; pour over chicken in slow cooker. Cover and cook on LOW 2 hours.

**3.** Combine cornstarch and 2 Tbsp. water, stirring until smooth. Stir into mixture in slow cooker. Stir in broccoli, edamame, and water chestnuts. Cover and cook on LOW 1 hour.

**4.** Sprinkle with green onions. Serve over rice. Top with cashews and chow mein noodles, if desired.

**ideal slow cooker:**
4- or 5-quart

*menu idea*
**for 6 to 8**

Chicken Chow Mein
Hot cooked rice
Mandarin oranges

*groceries needed...*

Check staples: pepper, vegetable oil, cornstarch

* 1 red bell pepper, cut into strips
* 2 lb. chicken breast tenders or 2 lb. skinned and boned chicken breasts, cut into strips
* 1 (5-oz.) bottle lite soy sauce
* 1 (11-oz.) bottle oyster sauce
* 1 bottle dark sesame oil
* 1 piece fresh ginger
* 1 (12-oz.) package frozen broccoli cuts
* 1 (12-oz.) package frozen edamame (green soybeans)
* 2 (8-oz.) cans sliced water chestnuts, drained
* 1 bunch green onions
* 1 (32-ounce) box converted rice
* ½ cup cashews (optional)
* 1 (3-oz.) can chow mein noodles (optional)

*side...*

* 2 (11-oz.) cans mandarin oranges

*menu idea*
### for 4

Chicken With
Artichokes and
Wild Mushrooms

Hot cooked orzo

Breaded broiled
tomato halves

*groceries needed...*

Check staples: flour, salt, pepper, olive oil

* 1 whole chicken
* 2 (4-oz.) packages assorted wild mushrooms
* 3 Vidalias or other sweet onions
* 1 (14-oz.) can chicken broth
* 1 (3.5-oz.) jar capers
* 1 (12-oz.) jar marinated artichoke hearts
* Fresh oregano leaves (optional)

*sides...*

* 1 (16-oz.) bag orzo
* 2 tomatoes
* 1 box breadcrumbs
* 1 container shredded Parmesan cheese
* 1 bunch fresh parsley

**Shopping Secret: We suggest purchasing a whole chicken for this recipe and getting the butcher to cut it up into pieces for you.**

# Chicken With Artichokes and Wild Mushrooms

hands-on time: 15 min. • total time: 4 hr., 15 min.
makes 4 servings

2   bone-in, skinned chicken breasts
2   chicken drumsticks
2   bone-in, skinned chicken thighs
3   Tbsp. all-purpose flour
1   tsp. salt
½   tsp. freshly ground pepper
3   Tbsp. olive oil
2   (4-oz.) packages assorted wild mushrooms
2¾  cups vertically sliced Vidalia or other sweet onion
1   cup chicken broth
3   Tbsp. drained capers
1   (12-oz.) jar marinated artichoke hearts, undrained
Garnish: fresh oregano leaves

1. Rinse chicken, and pat dry. Combine flour, salt, and pepper in a large zip-top plastic freezer bag. Place chicken pieces in bag; seal bag, and shake to coat. Remove chicken.

2. Heat oil in a large skillet over medium-high heat until hot; add chicken. Cook 3 minutes on each side or until lightly browned. Place chicken in a greased 5-qt. oval slow cooker, reserving drippings in skillet.

3. Cook mushrooms and onion in hot drippings 5 minutes or until tender. Add mushroom mixture, broth, capers, and artichokes to slow cooker. Cover and cook on LOW 4 hours or until chicken is tender. Garnish, if desired.

# Rosemary Chicken Lasagna

hands-on time: 13 min. • total time: 3 hr., 13 min.
makes 8 to 10 servings

2    Tbsp. olive oil

1½  to 2 Tbsp. chopped fresh rosemary

1    Tbsp. jarred minced garlic

1    cup frozen prechopped onion

4    cups chopped cooked chicken

Freshly ground pepper

2    (15-oz.) jars Alfredo sauce

1    (9-oz.) box no-boil lasagna noodles

1    (15-oz.) container ricotta cheese

1    (8-oz.) container sour cream

1    large egg, lightly beaten

½    tsp. freshly ground pepper

4    cups (16 oz.) shredded mozzarella cheese

½    cup coarsely chopped pitted kalamata olives

Garnish: fresh rosemary

1. Heat oil in a large skillet over medium-high heat. Sauté rosemary and garlic in hot oil 1 minute or until very fragrant. Add onion; sauté 4 to 5 minutes or until browned. Remove from heat; stir in chicken. Sprinkle with desired amount of pepper.

2. Spread 1 cup Alfredo sauce in bottom of a lightly greased 5-qt. oval slow cooker. Arrange 6 uncooked noodles over sauce, breaking noodles as needed to fit in slow cooker. Top with one-third of chicken mixture.

3. Combine ricotta cheese and next 3 ingredients in a bowl. Spread 1 cup ricotta mixture over chicken mixture. Sprinkle with 1 cup mozzarella. Repeat these layers twice: 1 cup Alfredo sauce, 5 lasagna noodles, half each of remaining chicken mixture, remaining ricotta mixture, and remaining mozzarella.

4. Cover and cook on LOW 3 hours. Top with olives before serving. Garnish, if desired.

## ideal slow cooker:
### 5-quart oval

## menu idea
### for 8 to 10

**Rosemary Chicken Lasagna**

**Salad greens**

**Breadsticks**

## groceries needed...

Check staples: olive oil, minced garlic, pepper, eggs, salad dressing

- 1 bunch fresh rosemary
- 1 (8-oz.) package frozen prechopped onion
- 4 cups chopped cooked chicken
- 2 (15-oz.) jars Alfredo sauce
- 1 (9-oz.) box no-boil lasagna noodles (we tested with Barilla)
- 1 (15-oz.) container ricotta cheese
- 1 (8-oz.) container sour cream
- 4 cups (16 oz.) shredded mozzarella cheese
- 1 large can pitted kalamata olives

## sides...

- 2 (8-oz.) bags mixed salad greens
- 2 tomatoes
- 1 package breadsticks

**Slow-Cooker Secret:** Pick up a box of slow cooker liners at the grocery—they come 4 to a box. The convenience of a lined pot is worth it for this chicken dressing that gets crusty around the outside as it cooks. Prepare the chicken in advance—the easiest option is to shred the meat from a warm rotisserie chicken.

*ideal slow cooker:*
5- or 6-quart

*menu idea*
for 8 to 10

Chicken and
Cranberry Dressing

Whole-berry
cranberry sauce

Roasted
Brussels sprouts

# Chicken and Cranberry Dressing

**hands-on time: 15 min.** • **total time: 7 hr., 15 min.**
**makes 8 to 10 servings**

| | |
|---|---|
| 1 | slow cooker liner |
| 6 | cups crumbled cornbread |
| 4 | cups chopped or shredded cooked chicken |
| 2 | cups frozen chopped celery, onion, and bell pepper mix |
| 1½ | cups dried cranberries or cherries |
| 8 | slices firm white bread, torn into bite-size pieces |
| 3 | large eggs, lightly beaten |
| 2 | (14-oz.) cans chicken broth |
| 2 | (10¾-oz.) cans cream of chicken soup |
| ½ | tsp. freshly ground pepper |
| ⅓ | cup butter |

1. Place a slow cooker liner in a 5- or 6-qt. slow cooker. Coat liner with cooking spray. Place cornbread in liner. Add chicken and next 7 ingredients; toss gently. Dot with butter.

2. Cover and cook on HIGH 4 hours or on LOW 7 hours or until dressing is puffed and set in center. Rotate slow cooker insert halfway after 2 hours. Stir before serving.

*groceries needed...*

Check staples: eggs, pepper, butter

- 1 package slow cooker liners
- Cornbread
- 4 cups chopped or shredded cooked chicken
- 2 (8-oz.) packages frozen chopped celery, onion, and bell pepper mix (we tested with McKenzie's)
- 1 (6-oz.) package dried cranberries
- 1 package white bread
- 2 (14-oz.) cans chicken broth
- 2 (10¾-oz.) cans cream of chicken soup

*sides...*

- 1 can whole berry cranberry sauce
- 2 lb. Brussels sprouts

**menu idea**
for 8 to 10

**Chicken Tetrazzini**

**Steamed zucchini**

**Broiled tomato halves topped with breadcrumbs and Parmesan cheese**

**groceries needed...**

Check staples: butter, flour, milk, salt, pepper

- 1 (8-oz.) package sliced fresh mushrooms
- 1 onion
- 1 bottle Marsala
- 1 (12-oz.) package spaghetti
- 4 cups chopped cooked chicken
- 1 package slivered almonds
- 8 oz. Parmigiano-Reggiano cheese

**sides...**

- 2 lb. zucchini
- 4 or 5 tomatoes
- 1 box breadcrumbs
- 1 container shredded Parmesan cheese

**Substitution Secret: Leftover turkey can be used instead of chicken, if desired. You can also substitute dry sherry for the Marsala.**

# Chicken Tetrazzini

hands-on time: 15 min. • total time: 4 hr., 25 min.
makes 8 to 10 servings

½ cup butter, divided

1 (8-oz.) package sliced fresh mushrooms

1 onion, chopped

½ cup all-purpose flour

4 cups milk

¼ cup Marsala

½ tsp. salt

½ tsp. freshly ground pepper

12 oz. uncooked spaghetti, broken in half

4 cups chopped cooked chicken

½ cup slivered almonds, toasted

2 cups freshly grated Parmigiano-Reggiano cheese, divided

1. Melt 2 Tbsp. butter in a large deep skillet over medium-high heat. Add mushrooms and onion; sauté 3 to 4 minutes or until tender. Remove mushroom mixture, and set aside.

2. Melt remaining 6 Tbsp. butter in skillet; whisk in flour until smooth. Cook 1 minute, whisking constantly. Gradually whisk in milk; bring to a boil. Cook 2 to 3 minutes or until mixture thickens, stirring constantly. Stir in Marsala, salt, and pepper.

3. Spoon one-third of white sauce into a 5- or 6-quart slow cooker. Top with half of spaghetti, half of mushroom mixture, half of chicken, half of almonds, and half of cheese. Repeat layers with one-third of white sauce, remaining spaghetti, mushroom mixture, chicken, and almonds. Top with remaining white sauce; sprinkle with remaining cheese. Cover and cook on LOW 4 hours. Let stand 10 minutes before serving.

**Slow-Cooker Secret: Be sure not to add the sour cream until the dish has finished cooking. Dairy products can curdle if exposed to high heat for very long.**

# Hungarian Chicken With Smoked Paprika

hands-on time: 12 min. • total time: 8 hr., 22 min.
makes 4 servings

1   red bell pepper, cored, seeded, and sliced
1   yellow bell pepper, cored, seeded, and sliced
1   onion, sliced
1   (28-oz.) can diced tomatoes, drained, with ½ cup juice reserved
1   cup chicken broth, divided
1   garlic clove, minced
1   tsp. picante Spanish smoked paprika or 1½ tsp. Hungarian paprika
1   Tbsp. plus 2 tsp. olive oil
1   (3-lb.) chicken, quartered and skinned
1   Tbsp. kosher salt
½   tsp. pepper
⅓   cup sour cream
Hot cooked pasta

**1.** Place peppers, onion, tomatoes, ½ cup broth, garlic, and paprika in a 6-qt. slow cooker. Heat oil in a large skillet over medium-high heat. Sprinkle chicken with salt and pepper. Add to skillet, and cook for 8 minutes or until browned. Transfer to slow cooker. Pour remaining ½ cup broth in skillet; cook 2 minutes, stirring to loosen particles from bottom of skillet. Pour liquid into slow cooker, and cook on HIGH for 6 hours.

**2.** Remove chicken, and let cool. Remove meat from bones, and return meat to slow cooker; discard bones. Stir in sour cream. Serve chicken over hot cooked pasta.

*menu idea*
for 4

Hungarian Chicken
With Smoked Paprika

Egg noodles

Steamed broccoli

*groceries needed...*

Check staples: olive oil, kosher salt, pepper

* 1 red bell pepper
* 1 yellow bell pepper
* 1 onion
* 1 (28-oz.) can diced tomatoes
* 1 (14-oz.) can chicken broth
* 1 garlic bulb
* Picante Spanish smoked paprika or Hungarian paprika
* 1 (3-lb.) chicken
* 1 (8-oz.) container sour cream

*sides...*

* 1 (12-oz.) package egg noodles
* 1 bunch broccoli

*ideal slow cooker:*

**5-quart oval**

*menu idea*

**for 4**

Lemon-Rosemary
Chicken

**Brown rice**

**Steamed
vegetables**

*groceries needed...*

Check staples: butter, salt, pepper

* 1 (4-lb.) chicken
* 2 lemons
* 1 bunch fresh rosemary
* 1 garlic bulb

*sides...*

* 1 (14-oz.) box instant brown rice
* 1 (12-oz.) package fresh frozen
  steaming vegetables

**Slow-Cooker Secret: Rather than removing the slow cooker lid to check on the chicken, it's best to gently tap the lid to release the condensation so you can see inside.**

# Lemon-Rosemary Chicken

hands-on time: 7 min.  •  total time: 4 hr., 49 min.
makes 4 servings

1   (4-lb.) chicken

1   lemon

3   sprigs fresh rosemary

2   garlic cloves

3   Tbsp. unsalted butter, divided

Salt and pepper

Garnish: lemon wedges, fresh rosemary

1. Rinse chicken, and pat dry. Cut lemon in half, and place inside cavity of chicken; add rosemary, garlic, and 2 Tbsp. butter. Fold wingtips under chicken, and tie legs together with string. Sprinkle chicken with salt and pepper.

2. Place chicken, breast side up, on a small rack inside a 5-qt. oval slow cooker. Cook on HIGH for 4 to 4½ hours or until an instant-read thermometer inserted into thigh registers 170°.

3. Preheat broiler. Melt remaining 1 Tbsp. butter. Transfer chicken, breast side up, to a foil-lined baking sheet. Brush chicken with melted butter, and broil to brown skin 2 to 3 minutes. Let stand 10 minutes on a cutting board before carving and serving. Garnish, if desired.

*menu idea*

for 4

**Creamy Thyme
Chicken and Winter
Vegetables**

**Hot cooked rice**

**Lime sherbet**

*groceries needed...*

Check staples: salt, dried thyme,
pepper, breadcrumbs

- 8 chicken thighs
- 1 (8-oz.) package frozen
  prechopped onion
- 1 lb. Yukon gold potatoes
- 1 lb. sweet potatoes
- 1 lb. rutabagas
- 2 (10¾-oz.) cans cream of
  chicken soup
- 4 oz. goat cheese
- 1 bunch fresh thyme (optional)

*sides...*

- 1 (14-oz.) package boil-in-bag rice
- ½ gal. lime sherbet

Slow-Cooker Secret: Slow cooking
root vegetables beneath juicy chicken
thighs allows meat juices to drip down
and impart great flavor.

# Creamy Thyme Chicken and Winter Vegetables

hands-on time: 15 min. • total time: 5 hr., 15 min.
makes 4 servings

| | |
|---|---|
| 8 | chicken thighs, skinned |
| 1 | (8-oz.) package frozen prechopped onion |
| 1 | lb. Yukon gold potatoes, peeled and sliced |
| 1 | lb. sweet potatoes, peeled and sliced |
| 1 | lb. rutabagas, peeled and sliced |
| 2 | (10¾-oz.) cans cream of chicken soup |
| 1 | tsp. salt |
| ½ | tsp. dried thyme |
| ½ | tsp. pepper |
| 4 | oz. goat cheese |
| ½ | cup Italian-seasoned breadcrumbs |

Garnish: fresh thyme

1. Preheat broiler. Place chicken on a lightly greased rack in an aluminum foil-lined broiler pan. Broil 5½ inches from heat 10 minutes.

2. Meanwhile, layer onion, potatoes, and rutabaga in a 6-qt. slow cooker. Stir together soup and next 3 ingredients in a medium bowl; pour over vegetables. Top with chicken.

3. Combine cheese and breadcrumbs. Sprinkle over chicken. Cover and cook on LOW 5 hours or until vegetables are tender. Garnish, if desired.

## Plum-Glazed Chicken With Caramelized Shallots

hands-on time: 15 min. • total time: 6 hr., 15 min.
makes 4 servings

| | |
|---|---|
| 8 | chicken thighs (about 3 lb.) |
| ½ | tsp. salt, divided |
| ½ | tsp. freshly ground pepper, divided |
| 2 | Tbsp. butter |
| 8 | large shallots, peeled |
| ¼ | cup Calvados or apple brandy |
| 1 | cup dried pitted plums |
| ½ | cup chicken broth |
| 2 | tsp. chopped fresh thyme |

Garnish: fresh thyme sprigs

**1.** Preheat broiler. Sprinkle chicken with ¼ tsp. salt and ¼ tsp. pepper. Place chicken, skin side up, on a lightly greased rack of a lightly greased broiler pan. Broil 5½ inches from heat 10 minutes or until browned. Transfer chicken to a 5-qt. slow cooker.

**2.** Meanwhile, melt butter in a large skillet over medium-high heat. Add shallots; cook 8 minutes or until caramelized, turning occasionally. Add brandy, and cook 2 minutes or until liquid is reduced by half, stirring to loosen particles from bottom of skillet.

**3.** Add shallot mixture, remaining ¼ tsp. salt, ¼ tsp. pepper, plums, chicken broth, and chopped thyme to chicken in slow cooker. Cover and cook on LOW 6 hours or until chicken is tender. Garnish, if desired.

*ideal slow cooker:*
5-quart

*menu idea*
for 4

**Plum-Glazed Chicken With Caramelized Shallots**

**Wild rice blend**

**Steamed haricots verts**

*groceries needed...*

Check staples: salt, pepper, butter
* 3 lb. chicken thighs
* 8 shallots
* Bottle of Calvados or apple brandy
* 10-oz. package dried pitted plums
* 1 (14-oz.) can chicken broth
* 1 bunch fresh thyme

*sides...*

* 1 (6-oz.) package long grain and wild rice mix
* 1½ lb. haricots verts

*menu idea*

### for 4 to 6

**Slow-Cooker
Orange Chicken
With Potatoes**

**Steamed
asparagus**

*groceries needed...*

Check staples: kosher salt, pepper,
jarred minced garlic, honey

* 8 chicken thighs
* 1 onion
* 1 lb. small red potatoes
* 1 small butternut squash
* 1 orange
* 1 (14-oz.) can low-sodium
  chicken broth
* 1 bunch fresh thyme

*side...*

* 1 bunch asparagus

**Slow-Cooker Secret: Typically, vegetables do not cook as quickly as meat does, so they should be placed in the slow cooker first, closer to the heating element.**

# Slow-Cooker Orange Chicken With Potatoes

hands-on time: 12 min. • total time: 2 hr., 42 min.
makes 4 to 6 servings

| | |
|---|---|
| 8 | chicken thighs, skinned |
| 1 | tsp. kosher salt |
| 1/2 | tsp. pepper |
| 1 | onion, cut into eighths |
| 1 | lb. small red potatoes, halved |
| 1 | small butternut squash, peeled, seeded, and cut into 1-inch pieces |
| 1 | tsp. jarred minced garlic |
| 1 | orange, cut into 1/4-inch rings |
| 1 | cup low-sodium chicken broth |
| 1 | Tbsp. honey |
| 8 | sprigs thyme |

**1.** Pat chicken dry with paper towels, and season with salt and pepper. Brown chicken in a large skillet over medium-high heat 4 minutes on each side.

**2.** Combine onion, potato, chicken, and remaining ingredients in a 6-qt. slow cooker. Cover and cook on HIGH 2½ hours or on LOW 5 hours.

**Substitution Secret:** Substitute an extra ¼ cup chicken broth in place of wine, if you prefer.

# Braised Chicken Thighs With Carrots and Potatoes

hands-on time: 11 min. · total time: 7 hr., 11 min.
makes 6 servings

1 medium onion, halved lengthwise and sliced
4 medium-size new potatoes (about 1 lb.), cut into ¼-inch-thick slices
1 lb. baby carrots
1¼ tsp. salt, divided
½ tsp. pepper, divided
¼ cup chicken broth
¼ cup dry white wine
1 tsp. jarred minced garlic
½ tsp. dried thyme
1 tsp. paprika
1½ lb. chicken thighs, skinned
Garnish: fresh thyme

**1.** Place onion in a lightly greased 6-qt. slow cooker; top with potatoes and carrots. Combine ¾ tsp. salt, ¼ tsp. pepper, broth, and next 3 ingredients. Pour broth mixture over vegetables. Combine paprika, remaining ½ tsp. salt, and remaining ¼ tsp. pepper; rub over chicken thighs, and arrange on top of vegetables.

**2.** Cover and cook on HIGH 1 hour and LOW 6 hours or until chicken and vegetables are tender. Garnish, if desired.

*menu idea*
for 6

Braised Chicken Thighs With Carrots and Potatoes

Roasted green beans

*groceries needed...*

Check staples: salt, pepper, jarred minced garlic, dried thyme, paprika
✳ 1 medium onion
✳ 4 medium-size new potatoes
✳ 1 lb. baby carrots
✳ 1 (14 oz.) can chicken broth
✳ Dry white wine
✳ 1½ lb. chicken thighs
✳ 1 bunch fresh thyme (optional)

*side...*
✳ 1½ lb. green beans

*menu idea*
**for 4**

**Mediterranean Chicken With Olives and Tomatoes**

**Rice**

**French bread**

*groceries needed...*

Check staples: kosher salt, pepper, jarred minced garlic

* 4 chicken leg quarters (about 4 lb.)
* 1 small lemon
* 1 can pimiento-stuffed Spanish olives, halved
* 1 can pitted kalamata olives, halved
* 1 bunch fresh thyme
* 1 (14½-oz.) can diced tomatoes with basil, garlic, and oregano
* 1 (4-oz.) package crumbled feta cheese

*sides...*

* 1 (16-oz.) package rice
* 1 loaf French bread

# Mediterranean Chicken With Olives and Tomatoes

hands-on time: 13 min. • total time: 3 hr., 13 min.
makes 4 servings

4   chicken leg quarters (about 4 lb.)
1   tsp. kosher salt
½   tsp. freshly ground pepper
1   small lemon
½   cup pimiento-stuffed Spanish olives, halved
½   cup pitted kalamata olives, halved
1   Tbsp. chopped fresh thyme
2   Tbsp. jarred minced garlic
1   (14½-oz.) can diced tomatoes with basil, garlic, and oregano, undrained
3   oz. feta cheese, crumbled (optional)

**1.** Rinse chicken, and pat dry. Sprinkle chicken with salt and pepper. Heat a large nonstick skillet over medium-high heat. Add chicken to pan; cook 3 minutes on each side or until browned. Transfer chicken to a 5-qt. slow cooker, discarding drippings.

**2.** Grate zest, and squeeze juice from lemon to measure 1 tsp. and 1 Tbsp., respectively. Stir together lemon zest, lemon juice, olives, and next 3 ingredients in a medium bowl. Pour over chicken. Cover and cook on LOW 3 hours or until chicken is tender. Sprinkle chicken with cheese, if desired.

**Shopping Secret:** Look for Sriracha hot chili sauce with Asian foods on the grocery shelves. It's a staple on the kitchen table in parts of Asia—much like ketchup is in the states. The blend of chilies, garlic, sugar, salt, and vinegar is very spicy.

## Spicy Asian Barbecued Drummettes

hands-on time: 8 min. • total time: 3 hr., 8 min.
makes 2 to 4 servings

3  lb. chicken drummettes (about 20)
½  tsp. salt
¼  tsp. pepper
1  cup honey-barbecue sauce
1  Tbsp. Sriracha hot chili sauce
1  Tbsp. soy sauce
3  garlic cloves, pressed
Garnish: toasted sesame seeds, sliced green onions (optional)

**1.** Preheat broiler.

**2.** Sprinkle drummettes with salt and pepper. Place on a lightly greased rack in a broiler pan. Broil 3 inches from heat 8 minutes or until browned. Place drummettes in a 4-qt. slow cooker.

**3.** Combine barbecue sauce and next 3 ingredients; pour over drummettes. Cover and cook on LOW 3 hours. Sprinkle with sesame seeds and sliced green onions, if desired. Serve with sauce for dipping.

*ideal slow cooker:*
4-quart

*menu idea*
for 2 to 4

Spicy Asian Barbecued Drummettes

French fries

Cucumber spears

*groceries needed...*
Check staples: salt, pepper, soy sauce
❋ 3 lb. chicken drummettes (about 20)
❋ 1 (18-oz.) bottle honey-barbecue sauce (we tested with Kraft)
❋ 1 (17-oz.) bottle Sriracha hot chili sauce
❋ 1 bulb garlic
❋ 1 small bottle sesame seeds (optional)
❋ 1 bunch green onions (optional)

*sides...*
❋ 1 (32-oz.) package frozen French fries
❋ 1 or 2 cucumbers

*menu idea*

### for 4

**Peach-Ginger Wings**

**Sugar snap peas**

*groceries needed...*

Check staples: soy sauce, hot sauce, jarred minced garlic

- 4 lb. halved chicken wings (about 32 wing pieces)
- 1 (18-oz.) jar peach preserves (we tested with Smucker's)
- 1 piece fresh ginger
- 1 small can frozen limeade concentrate

*side...*

- 1 lb. sugar snap peas

**Shopping Secret: Some meat markets sell wings already halved. If yours doesn't, ask the butcher to halve them for you to save time.**

# Peach-Ginger Wings

hands-on time: 15 min. • total time: 4 hr., 15 min.
makes 4 servings

| | |
|---|---|
| 4 | lb. halved chicken wings (about 32 wing pieces) |
| 1 | cup peach preserves |
| ½ | cup soy sauce |
| 2 | Tbsp. grated fresh ginger |
| 1 | Tbsp. frozen limeade concentrate, thawed |
| 1 | tablespoon jarred minced garlic |
| ¼ | tsp. hot sauce |

1. Preheat broiler. Place wings on a lightly greased rack in a lightly greased broiler pan. Broil 3 inches from heat 14 minutes or until browned. Transfer wings to a lightly greased 5-qt. slow cooker.

2. While wings broil, stir together preserves and remaining ingredients in a small bowl. Pour peach mixture over wings. Cover and cook on LOW 4 hours.

**ideal slow cooker:**
5-quart

**menu idea**
for 6 to 8

Open-Faced
Sloppy Toms
**Sweet potato fries**
**Lemonade**

# Open-Faced Sloppy Toms

hands-on time: 12 min. • total time: 6 hr., 12 min.
makes 6 to 8 servings

| | |
|---|---|
| 2 | lb. ground turkey |
| 2 | (8-oz.) packages frozen chopped celery, onion, and bell pepper mix |
| 1 | Tbsp. jarred minced garlic |
| 1 | (15-oz.) can tomato sauce |
| 1 | (6-oz.) can tomato paste |
| 1/3 | cup firmly packed light brown sugar |
| 1/4 | cup cider vinegar |
| 2 | Tbsp. Worcestershire sauce |
| 2 | tsp. paprika |
| 1/2 | tsp. chili powder |
| 1/2 | tsp. salt |
| 1/2 | tsp. freshly ground pepper |
| 6 | to 8 slices Texas toast |

Garnish: finely chopped red onion, dill pickle slices

1. Brown first 3 ingredients in a large skillet over medium-high heat, stirring often, 10 minutes or until turkey crumbles and is no longer pink.

2. Meanwhile, combine tomato sauce and next 8 ingredients in a 5-qt. slow cooker. Stir turkey mixture into tomato sauce mixture. Cover and cook on LOW 6 hours.

3. Prepare Texas toast according to package directions. To serve, spoon turkey mixture over toast. Garnish, if desired.

**groceries needed...**

Check staples: jarred minced garlic, brown sugar, Worcestershire sauce, paprika, chili powder, salt, pepper, dill pickle slices

* 2 lb. ground turkey
* 2 (8-oz.) packages frozen chopped celery, onion, and bell pepper mix (we tested with McKenzie's)
* 1 (15-oz.) can tomato sauce
* 1 (6-oz.) can tomato paste
* 1 (16-oz.) bottle cider vinegar
* 1 (11.25-oz.) package Texas toast
* 1 red onion (optional)

**sides...**

* 1 (20-oz.) package frozen sweet potato fries
* Lemonade

*menu idea*

**for 8**

Mediterranean Roast
Turkey

Couscous

Brussels sprouts

*groceries needed...*

Check staples: olive oil, lemon juice,
jarred minced garlic, salt, pepper, flour

- 1 (4-lb.) boneless turkey breast
- 1 large onion
- 1 can pitted kalamata olives
- 1 package julienne-cut oil-packed
  sun-dried tomato halves
- Greek seasoning mix
- 1 (14-oz.) can chicken broth

*sides...*

- 2 (8.8-oz.) packages Israeli
  couscous
- 1½ lb. fresh Brussels sprouts or
  2 (10-oz.) packages frozen
  Brussels sprouts

**Ingredient Secret:** Buy frozen prechopped onion instead of chopping
your own to save time.

# Mediterranean Roast Turkey

**hands-on time: 13 min.** • **total time: 7 hr., 43 min.**
**makes 8 servings**

| | |
|---|---|
| 1 | Tbsp. olive oil |
| 1 | (4-lb.) boneless turkey breast, trimmed |
| 2 | cups chopped onion |
| ½ | cup pitted kalamata olives |
| ½ | cup julienne-cut oil-packed sun-dried tomato halves, drained |
| 2 | Tbsp. fresh lemon juice |
| 1½ | tsp. jarred minced garlic |
| 1 | tsp. Greek seasoning mix |
| ½ | tsp. salt |
| ¼ | tsp. freshly ground black pepper |
| ½ | cup chicken broth, divided |
| 3 | Tbsp. all-purpose flour |

**1.** Heat olive oil in a large skillet over medium-high heat. Add
turkey breast to skillet and brown on all sides, about 8 minutes.

**2.** Combine turkey, onion, and next 7 ingredients in a 6-qt.
slow cooker. Add ¼ cup chicken broth. Cover and cook on
LOW for 7 hours.

**3.** Combine remaining ¼ cup broth and flour in a small bowl;
stir with a whisk until smooth. Add broth mixture to slow
cooker. Cover and cook on LOW for 30 minutes. Cut turkey
into slices; serve with gravy.

# {quick-fix side dishes}

### Roasted Baby Carrots

Preheat oven to 400°. Combine 2 Tbsp. vegetable oil, ¼ tsp. pepper, and 16 baby carrots in a jelly-roll pan; toss to coat. Bake at 400° for 25 minutes or until tender, stirring every 10 minutes.

### Fried Brown Rice

Sauté ½ cup sliced green onions and 2 minced garlic cloves in 1 Tbsp. vegetable oil. Add 1 beaten egg; cook over medium-low heat, stirring to scramble. Add 2 cups cooked brown rice and 2 Tbsp. soy sauce; cook, stirring frequently, until thoroughly heated.

## Marinated Cucumbers With Feta

Combine 3 large cucumbers, thinly sliced, and ¼ cup vinaigrette. Cover and chill. Sprinkle each serving with 1 Tbsp. crumbled feta cheese; sprinkle with freshly ground pepper, if desired.

# catch of the day

With flavors that are hard to beat, fish and shellfish offer a healthy option for weeknight fare. ❋ Fish and shellfish in the slow cooker generally boast shorter cooking times, just as they do with other cooking methods. ❋ Tasty favorites like Lemon Trout in Creamy White Wine Sauce, Greek Snapper, and Barbecued Shrimp make the ultimate weeknight meals.

**Slow-Cooker Secret: Trout fillets may overlap in the bottom of the slow cooker, but make sure the edges do not come in direct contact with the sides of the cooker and that they are covered with sauce so they won't dry out.**

*ideal slow cooker:*
4-quart

*menu idea*
for 4

Lemon Trout
in Creamy White
Wine Sauce

Haricots verts

Wild rice

Sliced heirloom
tomatoes

# Lemon Trout in Creamy White Wine Sauce

hands-on time: 5 min. · total time: 2 hr., 35 min.
makes 4 servings

1½ lb. trout fillets
½ tsp. salt, divided
½ tsp. freshly ground pepper, divided
¼ cup butter
1 tsp. jarred minced garlic
2 Tbsp. all-purpose flour
⅔ cup milk
⅓ cup dry white wine
1 Tbsp. lemon zest
1 Tbsp. sugar
Garnishes: lemon slices, chopped fresh parsley, capers

**1.** Sprinkle fish with ⅛ tsp. salt and ⅛ tsp. pepper, and arrange in bottom of a lightly greased 4-qt. slow cooker.

**2.** Melt butter in a small heavy saucepan over medium heat. Add garlic, and sauté 30 seconds. Whisk in flour until smooth. Cook 1 minute, whisking constantly. Gradually whisk in milk, wine, and zest; cook over medium heat, whisking constantly, until mixture is thickened and bubbly. Stir in remaining ⅜ tsp. salt, remaining ⅜ tsp. pepper, and sugar. Pour sauce over fish. Cover and cook on HIGH 2½ hours or just until fish flakes with a fork. Garnish, if desired.

*groceries needed...*

Check staples: salt, pepper, butter, jarred minced garlic, flour, milk, sugar

* 1½ lb. trout fillets
* ⅓ cup dry white wine
* 1 lemon
* 1 bunch fresh parsley
* 1 (3.5-oz.) jar capers

*sides...*

* 1 lb. haricots verts
* 1 (6.2-oz.) box long-grain and wild rice mix
* 2 tomatoes

*menu idea*

for 4

**Orange-Rosemary Poached Salmon**

**Orzo**

**Sautéed baby bok choy**

*groceries needed...*

Check staples: butter, salt, black pepper, red pepper

* 1 container orange juice
* 1 (14-oz.) can vegetable broth
* 1 bunch fresh parsley
* 1 garlic bulb
* 1 bunch fresh rosemary
* 1 navel orange
* 4 (6-oz.) skinless salmon fillets (½ to ¾ inch thick)

*sides...*

* 1 (16-oz.) package orzo
* 1 lb. baby bok choy

**Shopping Secret: Select fillets from the ends of the salmon. These are thinner and not as wide as those cut from the center of the fish.**

# Orange-Rosemary Poached Salmon

hands-on time: 9 min. • total time: 2 hr., 39 min.
makes 4 servings

1    cup orange juice

1    cup vegetable broth

½    cup fresh parsley leaves

3    Tbsp. butter

6    garlic cloves, pressed

2    (5-inch) sprigs fresh rosemary

1    navel orange, sliced

4    (6-oz.) skinless salmon fillets (½ to ¾ inch thick)

1    tsp. salt

2    tsp. orange zest

½    tsp. freshly ground black pepper

¼    tsp. ground red pepper

**1.** Place first 7 ingredients in a 5-qt. oval slow cooker. Cover and cook on HIGH 2 hours.

**2.** Meanwhile, sprinkle salmon with salt, orange zest, and peppers. Cover and chill.

**3.** Place salmon in liquid in slow cooker. Cover and cook 30 more minutes or until desired degree of doneness. Carefully transfer salmon to a serving platter using a large spatula.

**Slow-Cooker Secret:** Heating the poaching liquid on HIGH for 1 hour brings it to the perfect temperature to poach the fish in 2 hours. For best results, use an oval slow cooker because that size provides more surface area to arrange the fish in a single layer.

# Greek Snapper

**hands-on time: 9 min. • total time: 3 hr., 9 min.**
**makes 4 servings**

| | |
|---|---|
| 1½ | cups dry white wine |
| 1 | cup thinly sliced onion |
| 3 | garlic cloves, minced |
| 2 | bay leaves |
| 4 | (6-oz.) red snapper fillets (1 inch thick) |
| 4 | plum tomatoes, chopped |
| 1 | tsp. dried oregano |
| ½ | tsp. salt |
| ½ | tsp. freshly ground pepper |
| 1 | Tbsp. olive oil |
| 1 | oz. crumbled feta cheese |

Lemon wedges
Garnish: fresh oregano

**1.** Combine first 4 ingredients in a 6-qt. oval slow cooker. Cover and cook on HIGH 1 hour.

**2.** Add fish to slow cooker in a single layer. Combine tomato and next 3 ingredients in a bowl; spoon over fish. Drizzle olive oil over fish. Cover and cook on LOW 2 hours.

**3.** Carefully remove fish from cooking liquid. Serve over rice. Spoon tomato mixture over fish. Sprinkle with feta cheese, and serve with lemon wedges. Garnish, if desired.

*ideal slow cooker:*
**6-quart oval**

*menu idea*
**for 4**

Greek Snapper
Basmati rice
Grilled or roasted
asparagus

*groceries needed...*
Check staples: bay leaves, dried oregano, salt, pepper, olive oil

* 1 bottle dry white wine
* 1 onion
* 1 garlic bulb
* 4 (6-oz.) red snapper fillets (1 inch thick)
* 4 plum tomatoes
* 1 (4-oz.) package crumbled feta cheese
* 1 lemon
* 1 bunch fresh oregano

*sides...*
* 1 (6.5-oz.) box basmati rice
* 1 bundle asparagus

*groceries needed...*

Check staples: butter, jarred minced garlic, flour, salt, pepper, egg, salad dressing

* Parchment paper
* 1 onion
* 1 (8-oz.) package sliced baby portobello mushrooms
* 1 pt. half-and-half
* 1 (14-oz.) can chicken broth
* 1 (11-oz.) package frozen baby broccoli blend (we tested with Birds Eye)
* 1 (1-lb.) cod fillet
* ½ lb. fresh lump crabmeat
* 1 (17.3-oz.) package frozen puff pastry sheets
* 1 bottle dry sherry

*side...*

* 1 salad kit

# Seafood Pot Pie

**hands-on time: 15 min.** • **total time: 3 hr., 15 min.**
**makes 6 servings**

Parchment paper
¼   cup butter
1   cup chopped onion or 1 leek, thinly sliced
2   tsp. jarred minced garlic
1   (8-oz.) package sliced baby portobello mushrooms
¼   cup all-purpose flour
1   cup half-and-half
1   cup chicken broth
1   (11-oz.) package frozen baby broccoli blend
1   (1-lb.) cod fillet, cut into 2-inch pieces
½   lb. fresh lump crabmeat, drained and picked free of shell
½   tsp. each salt and freshly ground pepper
½   (17.3-oz.) package frozen puff pastry sheets, thawed
1   egg yolk, beaten
¼   cup dry sherry

**1.** To make a template for pastry lid, place a 3½-qt. slow cooker lid on parchment; trace lid shape. Remove lid. Cut out parchment shape, and set aside.

**2.** Melt butter in a large skillet over medium-high heat. Add onion, garlic, and mushrooms; sauté 5 minutes. Whisk in flour until smooth. Cook 1 minute, whisking constantly. Gradually whisk in half-and-half and broth; cook over medium heat, whisking constantly, until thickened and bubbly. Transfer to a slow cooker. Stir in vegetables. Cover and cook on LOW 2 hours. Uncover and stir in cod, crabmeat, salt, and pepper (cooker will be almost full). Cover and cook on HIGH 1 hour or until cod flakes with a fork.

**3.** Preheat oven to 400°. Roll out 1 pastry sheet on a lightly floured surface until smooth. Place parchment template on pastry, and cut out pastry using a paring knife. Place pastry on a parchment paper-lined baking sheet. Brush with egg yolk. Bake at 400° for 14 to 15 minutes. Stir sherry into pot pie. Top pot pie with pastry lid just before serving. Serve hot.

*ideal slow cooker:*

**6- or 7-quart oval**

*menu idea*
**for 4**

Crab Dip-Stuffed Mushrooms

Long-grain and wild rice

Zucchini and carrots

# Crab Dip-Stuffed Mushrooms

hands-on time: 11 min. • total time: 2 hr., 11 min.

makes 4 servings

- 1 lb. fresh lump crabmeat, drained
- 1 (8-oz.) package cream cheese, softened
- ⅓ cup sour cream
- ¼ cup mayonnaise
- 2 Tbsp. chopped fresh parsley
- 2 Tbsp. fresh lemon juice
- 1 tsp. Old Bay seasoning
- 2 tsp. Worcestershire sauce
- ¼ tsp. salt
- ¼ tsp. freshly ground pepper
- 4 large portobello mushrooms, stemmed
- 1 cup (4 oz.) shredded Swiss cheese

Garnishes: chopped fresh parsley, lemon wedges

1. Pick crabmeat, removing any bits of shell. Place cream cheese and next 8 ingredients in a bowl. Beat at medium speed with an electric mixer until blended; gently fold in crabmeat.

2. Scrape and discard brown gills from undersides of mushrooms, leaving edges of caps intact, using a spoon. Spoon crabmeat mixture into mushroom caps. Arrange mushrooms in a single layer in a lightly greased 6- to 7-qt. oval slow cooker. Sprinkle with cheese. Cover and cook on LOW 2 hours or until mushrooms are tender. Garnish, if desired.

*groceries needed...*

Check staples: mayonnaise, Worcestershire sauce, salt, pepper, Old Bay seasoning

- ✳ 1 lb. fresh lump crabmeat
- ✳ 1 (8-oz.) package cream cheese
- ✳ 1 (8-oz.) container sour cream
- ✳ 1 bunch fresh parsley
- ✳ 2 lemons
- ✳ 4 large portobello mushrooms
- ✳ 1 cup (4 oz.) shredded Swiss cheese

*sides...*

- ✳ 1 (6.2-oz.) box long-grain and wild rice mix
- ✳ ½ lb. zucchini
- ✳ 1 lb. carrots

*groceries needed...*

Check staples: Old Bay seasoning

- 12 small new potatoes (1¼ lb.)
- 1 (12-oz.) beer
- 1 bunch celery
- 1 onion
- 2 lemons
- 1 lb. kielbasa sausage
- 1 (12-ct.) package frozen corn on the cob (we tested with Green Giant Nibblers)
- 2 lb. unpeeled, large raw shrimp
- 1 (12-oz.) bottle cocktail sauce

*sides...*

- 1 loaf French bread
- ½ gallon vanilla ice cream

Slow-Cooker Secret: To make this South Carolina classic work in the slow cooker, you'll need the largest one available—a 7-qt. one. This is an easy dump-and-go recipe. Just pay attention to the times for adding the different ingredients.

# Lowcountry Boil

**hands-on time: 4 min. • total time: 5 hr., 34 min.**
**makes 6 servings**

12  small new potatoes (1¼ lb.)
1  (12-oz.) can beer
4  to 5 Tbsp. Old Bay seasoning
2  celery ribs, cut into 4-inch pieces
1  onion, quartered
2  lemons, halved
1  lb. kielbasa sausage, cut into 1-inch pieces
½  (12-ct.) package frozen corn on the cob (do not thaw)
2  lb. unpeeled, large raw shrimp
Cocktail sauce

1. Place potatoes in a 7-qt. slow cooker. Add 10 cups water, beer, and next 3 ingredients. Squeeze juice from lemon halves into mixture in slow cooker; add lemon halves to slow cooker. Cover and cook on LOW 3 hours.

2. Add sausage and corn. Cover and cook on LOW 2 hours. Add shrimp; stir gently. Cover and cook on HIGH 15 minutes or until shrimp turn pink. Turn off cooker; let stand 15 minutes. Drain. Serve with cocktail sauce.

**Slow-Cooker Secret: Allow this sauce base to lazily simmer away and develop rich flavor. Add shrimp during the last hour of cooking so it doesn't overcook. Serve with crusty French bread for sopping the zesty juices— which is, after all, the best part.**

*ideal slow cooker:*
**6-quart oval**

*menu idea*
for 4

**Barbecued Shrimp**
**Corn on the cob**
**French bread**

# Barbecued Shrimp

hands-on time: 5 min. • total time: 2 hr., 50 min.
makes 4 servings

| | |
|---|---|
| 6 | garlic cloves, pressed |
| 1 | cup butter, divided |
| ½ | cup Worcestershire sauce |
| ¼ | cup fresh lemon juice |
| ¼ | cup cocktail sauce |
| 1 | Tbsp. freshly ground pepper |
| 1½ | Tbsp. Old Bay seasoning |
| 1 | tsp. paprika |
| 1 | tsp. dried Italian seasoning |
| 2 | lb. unpeeled, large raw shrimp (21/25 count) |
| 1 | lemon, sliced |

Hot sauce (optional)

Lemon wedges (optional)

2   French bread baguettes, sliced

**1.** Sauté garlic in ¼ cup butter in a skillet over medium-high heat 2 minutes or until fragrant and lightly browned. Remove from heat; spoon into a 6-qt. oval slow cooker. Add remaining ¾ cup butter and next 7 ingredients. Cover and cook on LOW 2 hours.

**2.** Add shrimp and sliced lemon. Cover and cook on HIGH 45 minutes or until shrimp turn pink, stirring once after 30 minutes. Add hot sauce, if desired. Serve with lemon wedges and bread.

*groceries needed...*

Check staples: butter, Worcestershire sauce, pepper, paprika, dried Italian seasoning, hot sauce, Old Bay seasoning

❋ 1 garlic bulb
❋ 3 to 5 lemons
❋ 1 (12-oz.) bottle cocktail sauce
❋ 2 lb. unpeeled, large raw shrimp (21/25 count)

*sides...*

❋ 4 ears fresh corn
❋ 2 French bread baguettes

*ideal slow cooker:*

4- to 5-quart

*menu idea*

for 4 to 6

**Shrimp Creole**

**Rice**

**Oven-roasted okra**

**Deli corn muffins**

*groceries needed...*

Check staples: salt, pepper, bay leaves

* 1 package bacon
* 1 red bell pepper
* 1 (8-oz.) container refrigerated prechopped celery, onion, and bell pepper mix
* 1 garlic bulb
* 1 bunch fresh parsley
* 1 container Cajun seasoning
* 2 (14.5-oz.) cans stewed tomatoes
* 1½ lb. peeled and deveined large raw shrimp
* 2 (8.8-oz.) packages microwaveable long-grain rice

*sides...*

* 1 lb. fresh okra
* Deli cornbread muffins

**Slow-Cooker Secret: Cook shrimp just until they turn pink and opaque. If you want to peel and devein the shrimp yourself, you will need to purchase 2 pounds to allow for the weight of the shells.**

# Shrimp Creole

hands-on time: 8 min. • total time: 2 hr., 8 min.
makes 6 to 8 servings

4    bacon slices
½    cup chopped red bell pepper
1    (8-oz.) container refrigerated prechopped celery, onion, and bell pepper mix
3    garlic cloves, minced
2    Tbsp. chopped fresh parsley
1    tsp. Cajun seasoning
1    bay leaf
¼    tsp. salt
¼    tsp. freshly ground pepper
2    (14.5-oz.) cans stewed tomatoes
1½   lb. peeled and deveined large raw shrimp
Hot cooked rice
Garnish: chopped fresh parsley

1. Cook bacon over medium-high heat 4 to 5 minutes or until crisp; remove bacon, and drain on paper towels, reserving drippings in skillet. Crumble bacon. Add red bell pepper and celery mixture to skillet; sauté 3 to 4 minutes or until tender. Add garlic; sauté 1 minute. Combine vegetable mixture, crumbled bacon, parsley, and next 5 ingredients in a lightly greased 4- to 5-qt. slow cooker. Cover and cook on HIGH 1 hour.

2. Stir in shrimp. Cover and cook 45 minutes to 1 hour or until shrimp turn pink. Discard bay leaf. Serve over hot cooked rice. Garnish, if desired.

**Flavor Secret:** Lemon grass paste, made from pulverized lemon grass stalks, is key to the flavor of this recipe. It comes in a plastic tube and is found in the produce section.

*ideal slow cooker:*
**5-quart**

# Coconut Shrimp and Rice

hands-on time: 11 min.  •  total time: 3 hr., 26 min.
makes 4 to 6 servings

2½  cups chicken broth

2  cups uncooked converted rice

2  Tbsp. fish sauce

1  Tbsp. chopped fresh ginger

1  Tbsp. lemon grass paste

½  tsp. salt

2  garlic cloves, pressed

1  (13.5-oz.) can coconut milk

1  medium-size red bell pepper, sliced

1½  lb. peeled cooked shrimp

1  cup diagonally sliced fresh snow peas

Garnishes: lime wedges, chopped fresh cilantro

**1.** Combine first 9 ingredients and 1 cup water in a 5-qt. slow cooker. Cover and cook on LOW 3 hours or until liquid is absorbed and rice is tender.

**2.** Stir in shrimp and snow peas. Cover and cook 15 more minutes. Garnish, if desired.

*menu idea*
for 4 to 6

Coconut Shrimp
and Rice

Orange sorbet

Green tea

*groceries needed...*

Check staples: salt

- 2 (14-oz.) cans chicken broth
- 1 (16-oz.) package converted rice (we tested with Uncle Ben's)
- 1 bottle fish sauce
- 1 piece fresh ginger
- 1 tube lemon grass paste (we tested with Gourmet Garden)
- 1 garlic bulb
- 1 (13.5-oz.) can coconut milk
- 1 medium-size red bell pepper
- 1½ lb. cooked peeled shrimp (3 lb. raw in shell)
- ¾ lb. fresh snow peas
- 2 limes (optional)
- 1 bunch fresh cilantro (optional)

*sides...*

- ½ gallon orange sorbet
- 1 box green tea bags

menu idea
for 6

**Seafood Gumbo**

**Rice**

**French bread**

groceries needed...

Check staples: Worcestershire sauce,
kosher salt, dried thyme leaves

* 1 (12-oz.) package bacon slices
* 2 (8-oz.) containers refrigerated
  prechopped celery, onion, and
  green pepper
* 1 garlic bulb
* 1 (14-oz.) can chicken broth
* 1 (14-oz.) can diced tomatoes
* ¾ lb. large raw shrimp, peeled
  and deveined (1 lb. raw in shell)
* 1 lb. fresh or frozen crabmeat
* 1 (16-oz.) package frozen cut okra

sides...

* 2 (14-oz.) packages boil-in-bag
  rice
* 1 loaf French bread

Flavor secret: This recipe skips the tedious steps and hard-to-find spices of traditional gumbos without compromising any of the flavor. Serve over rice.

# Seafood Gumbo

**hands-on time: 15 min. • total time: 3 hr., 20 min.**
**makes 6 servings**

| | |
|---|---|
| ½ | lb. sliced bacon, diced |
| 2 | (8-oz.) containers refrigerated prechopped celery, onion, and green pepper |
| 2 | garlic cloves, minced |
| 2 | cups chicken broth |
| 1 | (14-oz.) can diced tomatoes |
| 2 | Tbsp. Worcestershire sauce |
| 2 | tsp. kosher salt |
| 1 | tsp. dried thyme leaves |
| ¾ | lb. large raw shrimp, peeled and deveined |
| 1 | lb. fresh or frozen crabmeat |
| 2 | cups frozen cut okra |

**1.** Cook bacon in a large skillet over medium heat until crisp. With a slotted spoon, transfer bacon to a 5-qt. slow cooker. Discard all but a thin coating of drippings in skillet. Add celery mixture and garlic to skillet, and cook over medium heat, stirring frequently, until the vegetables are tender, about 10 minutes.

**2.** Spoon vegetables into slow cooker; add broth, tomatoes, Worcestershire, salt, and thyme. Cover and cook on HIGH for 2 hours. Add shrimp, crabmeat, and okra, and cook 1 hour on LOW heat. Serve over hot cooked rice.

# Bouillabaisse

hands-on time: 9 min. • total time: 3 hr., 9 min.
makes 6 to 8 servings

1   small fennel bulb, thinly sliced
1   (8-oz.) container refrigerated prechopped celery, onion, and bell pepper mix
1   Tbsp. olive oil
2   (14.5-oz.) cans diced tomatoes with basil, garlic, and oregano, undrained
1   bay leaf
1   (8-oz.) bottle clam juice
1   cup dry white wine
½   tsp. salt
½   tsp. freshly ground pepper
3   lb. whitefish pieces
1½  lb. fresh mussels, scrubbed and debearded
1   lb. unpeeled, large raw shrimp
Garnishes: lemon wedges, chopped fresh parsley

**1.** Sauté fennel and celery mixture in hot oil in a large skillet over medium-high heat 3 to 4 minutes or until tender. Stir in tomatoes and bay leaf. Pour mixture into a lightly greased 6- to 7-qt. slow cooker. Stir in clam juice and next 3 ingredients. Cover and cook on HIGH 2 hours or until simmering.

**2.** Stir fish, mussels, and shrimp into broth mixture in slow cooker. Reduce heat to LOW. Cover and cook on LOW 1 hour or until seafood is done. Discard bay leaf. Spoon stew into large shallow bowls. Garnish, if desired.

## ideal slow cooker:
### 6- to 7-quart

## menu idea
### for 6 to 8

Bouillabaisse
Garlic-rubbed French bread toast

## groceries needed...

Check staples: olive oil, salt, pepper, bay leaves, jarred minced garlic

* 1 small fennel bulb
* 1 (8-oz.) container refrigerated prechopped celery, onion, and bell pepper mix
* 2 (14.5-oz.) cans diced tomatoes with basil, garlic, and oregano
* 1 (8-oz.) bottle clam juice
* 1 bottle dry white wine
* 3 lb. whitefish pieces
* 1½ lb. fresh mussels
* 1 lb. unpeeled, large raw shrimp
* 2 lemons (optional)
* 1 bunch fresh parsley (optional)

## side...
* 1 loaf French bread

groceries needed...

Check staples: vegetable oil, brown sugar, salt

* 2 large shallots
* 1 bottle dry white wine
* 1 (4-oz.) jar red curry paste (we tested with Thai Kitchen)
* 1 (13.5-oz.) can coconut milk
* 1 (8-oz.) bottle clam juice
* ½ lb. fresh green beans
* 1 lb. carrots
* 1 large red bell pepper
* 3 lb. mussels
* 1 bunch fresh basil
* 2 limes

side...

* 1 loaf French bread

**Ingredient Secret: Before cooking, discard any opened mussels or ones that are heavy for their size (they are filled with sand). After cooking, discard any mussels that have not opened.**

# Mussels With Red Curry and Vegetables

hands-on time: 11 min. • total time: 3 hr., 31 min.
makes 4 servings

| | |
|---|---|
| 2 | Tbsp. vegetable oil |
| 2 | large shallots, chopped |
| ¼ | cup dry white wine |
| 3 | Tbsp. light brown sugar |
| 3 | Tbsp. red curry paste |
| ¼ | tsp. salt |
| 1 | (13.5-oz.) can coconut milk |
| 1 | (8-oz.) bottle clam juice |
| ½ | lb. fresh green beans, trimmed and cut into 1-inch pieces |
| 4 | carrots, diced |
| 1 | large red bell pepper, seeded and cut into vertical strips |
| 3 | lb. mussels, scrubbed and debearded |
| 2 | Tbsp. thinly sliced fresh basil |

Lime wedges

1. Heat oil in a small skillet over medium heat. Add shallots, and sauté 3 minutes or until tender. Transfer shallots to a 5-qt. slow cooker. Whisk in wine and next 5 ingredients until blended. Stir in green beans, carrot, and bell pepper. Cover and cook on LOW 3 hours or until vegetables are tender.

2. Increase temperature to HIGH. Add mussels to slow cooker, spreading into even layers. Cover and cook on HIGH 20 minutes or until mussels open. Serve in shallow bowls. Sprinkle with fresh basil, and serve with lime wedges and French bread.

# {quick-fix salads}

### Fruit Salad With Light Balsamic Dressing

Combine 2 cups cubed honeydew melon, 1 cup quartered strawberries, and 1 cup raspberries. Whisk together ¼ cup olive oil, 2 Tbsp. white balsamic vinegar, 1 Tbsp. honey, and ¼ tsp. salt. Drizzle over fruit; toss gently to coat. Garnish with mint.

### Romaine Salad

In a large bowl, whisk together ¼ cup mayonnaise, 2 Tbsp. Dijon mustard, 4 tsp. fresh lemon juice, 2 tsp. red wine vinegar, and 4 minced garlic cloves. Add 16 cups torn romaine lettuce, tossing gently to coat.

## Gourmet Greens With Oranges and Raisins

Arrange 1½ cups gourmet salad greens on each of 6 plates. Top each serving with ⅓ cup mandarin orange slices and 2 Tbsp. golden raisins. Drizzle each serving with bottled balsamic vinaigrette.

# meatless mains

Enjoy a delicious vegetarian homestyle meal at the end of the day with one of these quick-and-easy favorites. **These recipes will delight the palate with twists on traditional favorites like Enchilada Casserole, Meatless Shepherd's Pie, and Veggie Chili and Potato Tot Nachos.** Grains, pastas, soy products, beans, eggs, and vegetables are the filling and versatile stars of these protein-packed dishes. Plus, they take only minutes to prepare.

# Savory Italian Vegetable Bread Pudding

hands-on time: 8 min. • total time: 3 hr., 23 min.
makes 6 servings

1   Tbsp. olive oil
1   large zucchini, cubed
1   red bell pepper, chopped
1   small onion, chopped
6   large eggs
1   cup half-and-half
1½  tsp. Dijon mustard
1   tsp. dried Italian seasoning
½   tsp. salt
¼   tsp. pepper
1   (9.5-oz.) package frozen mozzarella and Monterey Jack cheese Texas toast, cut into 1-inch cubes
1   cup (4 oz.) shredded Italian six-cheese blend

**1.** Heat a large skillet over medium-high heat. Add oil. Sauté zucchini and next 2 ingredients in hot oil 5 minutes or until crisp-tender.

**2.** Whisk together eggs and next 5 ingredients.

**3.** Layer half of Texas toast in a lightly greased 5-qt. slow cooker; top with half of zucchini mixture and ½ cup cheese. Repeat layers. Pour egg mixture over all ingredients. Cover and cook on LOW 3 hours and 15 minutes or until set.

*groceries needed...*

* 1 (16-oz.) package frozen whole kernel corn
* 1 (14-oz.) can low-sodium fat-free vegetable broth
* 1 container Cajun seasoning
* 1 garlic bulb
* 2 (16-oz.) cans red beans
* 1 (28-oz.) can diced tomatoes
* 1 (16-oz.) package frozen cut okra
* 1 large onion
* 1 (14-oz.) package brown rice

*side...*

* 1 loaf French bread

**Serving Secret: If you don't want to go meatless with this recipe, stir in leftover ham.**

# Slow-Cooker Cajun Succotash

hands-on time: 6 min. • total time: 4 hr., 6 min.
makes 8 servings

2    cups frozen whole kernel corn
1    (14-oz.) can low-sodium fat-free vegetable broth
1½  tsp. Cajun seasoning
3    garlic cloves, minced
2    (16-oz.) cans red beans, drained and rinsed
1    (28-oz.) can diced tomatoes, undrained
1    (16-oz.) package frozen cut okra
1    large onion, chopped
Hot cooked brown rice

**1.** Combine all ingredients, except rice, in a 5-qt. slow cooker. Cover and cook on LOW 4 hours. Serve over hot cooked brown rice.

# Vegetable Moussaka

hands-on time: 15 min. • total time: 8 hr., 15 min.
makes 8 to 10 servings

¼ cup butter

¼ cup all-purpose flour

3 cups milk

1½ cups (6 oz.) shredded Parmesan cheese, divided

2 large eggs

2 egg yolks

½ tsp. salt

½ tsp. freshly ground pepper

1 (1½-lb.) eggplant, peeled and cubed

1½ cups refrigerated presliced onion

1 (8-oz.) package sliced baby portobello mushrooms

1 (20-oz.) package refrigerated sliced potatoes

4 cups chunky spaghetti sauce

Garnish: fresh chopped parsley

**1.** Melt butter in a heavy saucepan over low heat; whisk in flour until smooth. Cook 2 minutes, whisking constantly. Gradually whisk in milk; cook over medium heat 3 to 4 minutes, whisking constantly, until mixture is thickened and bubbly. Stir in ½ cup Parmesan cheese. Gradually whisk together eggs, egg yolks, salt, and pepper in a medium bowl. Gradually stir about one-fourth of hot cheese mixture into egg mixture; add egg mixture to remaining hot cheese mixture, whisking constantly.

**2.** Arrange eggplant in bottom of a 7-qt. slow cooker. Layer onion, mushrooms, and potatoes over eggplant; pour spaghetti sauce over vegetables. Top with cheese sauce and remaining 1 cup cheese. Cover and cook on LOW 8 hours or until vegetables are tender. Garnish, if desired.

*ideal slow cooker:*
**7-quart**

*menu idea*
**for 8 to 10**

Vegetable Moussaka

Green peas

Orzo

Pita wedges

*groceries needed...*

Check staples: butter, flour, milk, eggs, salt, pepper

✳ 1 (6-oz.) package shredded Parmesan cheese

✳ 1 (1½-lb.) eggplant

✳ 1½ cups refrigerated presliced onion

✳ 1 (8-oz.) package sliced baby portobello mushrooms

✳ 1 (20-oz.) package refrigerated sliced potatoes

✳ 2 (28-oz.) jars chunky spaghetti sauce

✳ 1 bunch fresh parsley (optional)

*sides...*

✳ 2 (12-oz.) packages frozen green peas

✳ 1 (16-oz.) package orzo

✳ 1 (28-oz.) package pita bread

*menu idea*
**for 6**

Meatless
Shepherd's Pie

Tossed salad with
grape tomatoes

Rolls

*groceries needed...*

Check staples: flour, salad dressing

* 2 (12-oz.) packages frozen meat-less burger crumbles (we tested with Morningstar Farms)
* 1 (14.5-oz.) can diced tomatoes with basil, garlic, and oregano
* 1 (16-oz.) package frozen peas and carrots
* 1 jar dried minced onion
* 1 (24-oz.) package refrigerated sour cream and chive mashed potatoes (we tested with Simply Potatoes)
* 1 (8-oz.) package shredded sharp Cheddar cheese
* 1 bunch fresh chives (optional)

*sides...*

* 1 package mixed salad greens
* 1 pt. grape tomatoes
* 1 package dinner rolls

**Ingredient Secret: Keep meatless burger crumbles in the freezer to make preparing quick, healthful meals a snap. They are ready to add to your recipes—no browning required.**

# Meatless Shepherd's Pie

hands-on time: 8 min. • total time: 4 hr., 8 min.
makes 6 servings

2   (12-oz.) packages frozen meatless burger crumbles
2   Tbsp. all-purpose flour
1   (14.5-oz.) can diced tomatoes with basil, garlic, and oregano, undrained
1   (16-oz.) package frozen peas and carrots
1   tsp. dried minced onion
1   (24-oz.) package refrigerated sour cream and chive mashed potatoes
1   cup (4 oz.) shredded sharp Cheddar cheese
Garnish: fresh chives

**1.** Toss together burger crumbles and flour in a large bowl until crumbles are coated. Stir in tomatoes and next 2 ingredients. Spoon mixture into a lightly greased 4-qt. slow cooker.

**2.** Microwave potatoes 1 minute according to package directions; stir and spread over vegetable mixture in slow cooker. Cover and cook on LOW 4 hours. Increase heat to HIGH. Sprinkle cheese over potatoes; cover and cook 7 minutes or until cheese melts. Garnish, if desired.

**Slow-Cooker Secret: Potato tots replace chips as the base for these cheesy nachos. Keep the finished dish on warm setting up to 2 hours—the potato tots will begin to fall apart slightly after lengthy heating.**

# Veggie Chili and Potato Tot Nachos

hands-on time: 6 min. • total time: 3 hr., 6 min.
makes 8 to 10 servings

1    (22-oz.) package frozen potato tots
1    cup refrigerated prechopped onion
2    (15-oz.) cans vegetarian chili with beans
1    (12-oz.) package frozen meatless burger crumbles
3    cups (12 oz.) shredded Cheddar cheese, divided
½    cup drained pickled jalapeño pepper slices (optional)

1. Place half of potato tots in a lightly greased 4- or 5-qt. slow cooker. Combine onion, chili, and crumbles; stir well. Spoon chili mixture over potato tots. Sprinkle with 1½ cups cheese. Top with remaining potato tots. Cover and cook on LOW 3 hours.

2. Uncover and sprinkle with remaining 1½ cups cheese and, if desired, jalapeño slices.

*ideal slow cooker:*

4- or 5-quart

*menu idea*
**for 8 to 10**

**Veggie Chili and Potato Tot Nachos**

**Deli coleslaw**

**Corn chips**

*groceries needed...*

- 1 (22-oz.) package frozen potato tots (we tested with Alexia)
- 1 (8-oz.) container refrigerated prechopped onion
- 2 (15-oz.) cans vegetarian chili with beans
- 1 (12-oz.) package frozen meatless burger crumbles (we tested with Morningstar Farms)
- 1 (12-oz.) package shredded Cheddar cheese
- 1 (7-oz.) can pickled jalapeño pepper slices (optional)

*sides...*

- 2 pt. deli coleslaw
- 1 (9.25-oz.) bag corn chips

*menu idea*

**for 6**

Mediterranean
Soufflé Casserole

Veggie bacon strips

Cantaloupe and
red grapes

Orange juice

*groceries needed...*

Check staples: eggs, pepper

* 1 (12-oz.) jar roasted red bell peppers
* 1 (14-oz.) can quartered artichoke hearts
* 1 (4.5-oz) can sliced black olives
* 1 (4-oz.) package crumbled feta cheese
* 1 (5-oz.) can evaporated milk
* 1 (6-oz.) container Greek yogurt
* 1 bunch fresh basil

*sides...*

* 1 (5.25-oz.) package veggie bacon strips
* 1 cantaloupe
* 1 lb. red grapes
* 1 qt. orange juice

Serving Secret: You'll use partial cans of olives and artichoke hearts for this recipe. Plan on homemade pizza a few nights later to make good use of these leftovers.

# Mediterranean Soufflé Casserole

hands-on time: 7 min. • total time: 3 hr., 17 min.
makes 6 servings

1    (12-oz.) jar roasted red bell peppers, drained and chopped
1    cup quartered artichoke hearts, chopped
½    cup sliced black olives
1    cup crumbled feta cheese
¼    cup evaporated milk
2    Tbsp. plain Greek yogurt
9    large eggs, lightly beaten
Freshly ground pepper
2    Tbsp. chopped fresh basil

1. Layer roasted red pepper, chopped artichoke, and olives in a lightly greased 3- or 4-qt. slow cooker. Combine cheese and next 3 ingredients; stir well, and pour over vegetables in slow cooker. Sprinkle with pepper. Cover and cook on LOW 3 hours or just until egg is set in center.

2. Turn off cooker. Let stand, covered, 10 minutes. Sprinkle with basil before serving.

**Slow-Cooker Secret:** Quickly thaw sweet potatoes by snipping off the corner of the bag and microwaving at HIGH 3 minutes.

*ideal slow cooker:*
5-quart

# Sweet Potato Breakfast Bake

hands-on time: 9 min.  •  total time: 4 hr., 9 min.
makes 8 servings

2  Tbsp. butter, divided

1  (14-oz.) package soy sausage

6  large eggs

2  cups half-and-half

1  tsp. dried Italian seasoning

2  cups herb-seasoned stuffing mix

2  cups (8 oz.) shredded mozzarella cheese, divided

1  cup refrigerated prechopped onion

1  (24-oz.) package steam-and-mash frozen cut sweet potatoes, thawed

Garnish: chopped fresh parsley

**1.** Melt 1 Tbsp. butter in a large skillet over medium-high heat. Brown sausage in melted butter, stirring often, 5 to 6 minutes or until sausage crumbles and is browned.

**2.** Meanwhile, whisk together eggs and next 2 ingredients in a medium bowl.

**3.** Grease a 5-qt. slow cooker with remaining 1 Tbsp. butter. Stir together sausage, egg mixture, stuffing mix, 1 cup cheese, and next 2 ingredients in slow cooker. Top with remaining 1 cup cheese. Cover and cook on LOW 4 hours or until set and edges are browned. Garnish, if desired.

*menu idea*
for 8

**Sweet Potato Breakfast Bake**

**Sautéed apple rings**

**Orange juice**

*groceries needed...*

Check staples: butter, eggs, dried Italian seasoning

* 1 (14-oz.) package soy sausage (we tested with Gimme Lean)
* 1 pt. half-and-half
* 1 (1-lb.) package herb-seasoned stuffing mix (we tested with Pepperidge Farm)
* 1 (8-oz.) package shredded mozzarella cheese
* 1 (8-oz.) container refrigerated prechopped onion
* 1 (24-oz.) package steam-and-mash frozen cut sweet potatoes
* 1 bunch fresh parsley (optional)

*sides...*

* 4 apples
* 2 qt. orange juice

*groceries needed...*

Check staples: pepper

* 2 (15-oz.) jars Alfredo sauce (we tested with Gia Russa)
* 2 (9-oz.) packages refrigerated wild mushroom agnolotti pasta (we tested with Buitoni Riserva)
* 1 (5-oz.) package shredded Parmesan cheese
* 2 pt. grape tomatoes
* 1 (12-oz.) package walnut halves
* 1 (10-oz.) package baby spinach

*sides...*

* 2 (9.9-oz.) packages salad kits
* 1 French baguette

**Ingredient Secret: Agnolotti are square ravioli packets typically filled with meat and/or vegetables.**

# Wild Mushroom Pasta Alfredo With Walnuts

**hands-on time: 6 min.** • **total time: 2 hr., 6 min.**
**makes 8 servings**

2   (15-oz.) jars Alfredo sauce

2   (9-oz.) packages refrigerated wild mushroom agnolotti pasta

1   cup (4 oz.) shredded Parmesan cheese

4   cups grape tomatoes

1   cup walnut halves, toasted

Freshly ground pepper

4   cups baby spinach

Garnish: additional shredded Parmesan cheese

1. Spoon 1 cup Alfredo sauce into a lightly greased 3½- or 4-qt. slow cooker. Spread 1 package of pasta over sauce. Top with ½ cup cheese, 2 cups tomatoes, and ½ cup walnuts. Sprinkle with pepper. Repeat layers once. Top with 1 cup Alfredo sauce. Reserve remaining Alfredo sauce for other uses.

2. Cover and cook on HIGH 2 hours. Stir in spinach just before serving. Garnish, if desired.

*ideal slow cooker:*
**5-quart**

*menu idea*
**for 6**

**Slow-Cooker Eggplant and Tomato Sauce With Pasta**

**Garlic breadsticks**

# Slow-Cooker Eggplant and Tomato Sauce With Pasta

hands-on time: 10 min. • total time: 4 hr., 22 min.
makes 6 servings

1   (28-oz.) can diced tomatoes, drained
1   (6-oz.) can tomato paste
½   cup red wine or water
1   medium eggplant (about 1 lb.), cut into ½-inch cubes
1   onion, finely chopped
2   garlic cloves, finely chopped
1   teaspoon dried oregano
Salt
1   (16-oz.) package rotini pasta
Garnish: grated Parmesan cheese

**1.** Combine tomatoes, tomato paste, wine, eggplant, onion, garlic, oregano, and ½ tsp. salt in a 5-qt. slow cooker; cover and cook on LOW 4 hours or until eggplant is soft and sauce is thick.

**2.** Just before sauce is done, bring a large pot of salted water to boil over high heat. Add pasta, and cook until al dente, about 10 minutes. Drain pasta, and toss with sauce. Garnish, if desired.

*groceries needed...*

Check staples: dried oregano, salt

* 1 (28-oz.) can diced tomatoes
* 1 (6-oz.) can tomato paste
* 1 bottle red wine
* 1 medium eggplant (about 1 lb.)
* 1 onion
* 1 garlic bulb
* 1 lb. rotini pasta
* 1 (5-oz.) package shredded Parmesan cheese (optional)

*side...*

* 1 package garlic breadsticks

*menu idea*

for 6

**Slow-Cooker Lasagna**

**Caesar salad**

*groceries needed...*

Check staples: kosher salt, pepper

* 1 (28-oz.) can diced tomatoes
* 1 (28-oz.) jar chunky pasta sauce
* 1 garlic bulb
* 1 bunch fresh oregano
* 1 (16-oz.) container ricotta cheese
* 1 bunch fresh flat-leaf parsley
* 1 (5-oz.) package shredded Parmesan
* 1 (12-oz.) package lasagna noodles
* 1 bunch Swiss chard
* 1 (12-oz.) package shredded mozzarella cheese

*side...*

* 2 (9.9-oz.) packages Caesar salad kits

**Slow-Cooker Secret: If using a slow cooker smaller than 6 quarts, the cooking time may take an additional hour or more, and results may vary.**

# Slow-Cooker Lasagna

hands-on time: 15 min. • total time: 2 hr., 15 min.
makes 6 servings

| | |
|---|---|
| 1 | (28-oz.) can diced tomatoes, drained |
| 1 | (28-oz.) jar chunky pasta sauce |
| 3 | garlic cloves, finely chopped |
| ¼ | cup fresh oregano, chopped |
| ½ | tsp. kosher salt |
| ¾ | tsp. pepper, divided |
| 1 | (16-oz.) container ricotta cheese |
| ½ | cup fresh flat-leaf parsley, chopped |
| ½ | cup shredded Parmesan cheese |
| 1 | (12-oz.) package lasagna noodles |
| 1 | bunch Swiss chard, tough stems removed and torn into large pieces |
| 3 | cups (12 oz.) shredded mozzarella cheese |

1. In a medium bowl, combine tomatoes, sauce, garlic, oregano, ½ tsp. salt, and ½ tsp. pepper. In another medium bowl, combine ricotta, parsley, Parmesan cheese, and remaining ¼ tsp. pepper. Spoon ⅓ cup of the tomato mixture into a 6-qt. slow cooker.

2. Top with a single layer of noodles, breaking them to fit as necessary. Add half the Swiss chard. Dollop with one-third of ricotta mixture and one-third of remaining tomato mixture. Sprinkle with one-third of mozzarella cheese. Add another layer of noodles, and repeat with other ingredients. Finish with a layer of noodles and remaining ricotta mixture, tomato mixture, and mozzarella. Cover and cook on LOW for 2 to 3 hours or until noodles are tender.

# Pastitsio

hands-on time: 15 min. • total time: 3 hr., 15 min.

makes 4 to 6 servings

2½  cups uncooked ziti pasta

1¼  cups chopped onion

3  garlic cloves, minced

2  tsp. olive oil

1  (12-oz.) package frozen meatless burger crumbles, thawed

1½  cups puttanesca-flavored pasta sauce

½  tsp. apple pie spice

½  tsp. salt

¼  tsp. freshly ground pepper

1  (8-oz.) package feta cheese, coarsely crumbled

1  (15-oz.) jar Alfredo sauce

3  large eggs

⅓  cup (1½ oz.) shredded Parmesan cheese

Garnishes: sliced black olives, fresh oregano leaves

**1.** Cook pasta according to package directions, including salt, and drain.

**2.** Sauté onion and garlic in hot oil in a large skillet over medium heat 5 minutes or until tender. Remove pan from heat; stir in meatless crumbles and next 4 ingredients. Add pasta, stirring well. Gently stir in feta cheese.

**3.** Spoon mixture into a greased 4- to 5-qt. oval slow cooker. Whisk together Alfredo sauce and eggs in a bowl; pour over pasta mixture. Sprinkle Parmesan cheese over sauce. Cover and cook on LOW 3 hours or until lightly browned and bubbly. Garnish, if desired.

*menu idea*

**for 6**

Thyme-Scented White
Bean Cassoulet

Vanilla ice cream with
chocolate syrup

*groceries needed...*

Check staples: olive oil, dried thyme,
salt, pepper, bay leaves, butter

* 1 large onion
* 1 bunch carrots
* 1 (16-oz.) package fresh parsnips
* 1 garlic bulb
* 1 (15.8-oz.) can great Northern beans
* 1 (14-oz.) can vegetable broth
* 1 (28-oz.) can diced tomatoes
* 1 (24-oz.) package dry breadcrumbs
* 1 (5-oz.) package shredded Parmesan cheese
* 1 small package meatless Italian sausage (such as Boca)
* 1 bunch fresh parsley

*side...*

* ½ gallon vanilla ice cream
* 1 bottle chocolate syrup

# Thyme-Scented White Bean Cassoulet

hands-on time: 15 min. • total time: 8 hr., 15 min.
makes 6 servings

| | |
|---|---|
| 1 | Tbsp. olive oil |
| 1½ | cups chopped onion |
| 1½ | cups (½-inch-thick) slices diagonally cut carrot |
| 1 | cup (½-inch-thick) slices diagonally cut parsnips |
| 2 | garlic cloves, minced |
| 3 | cups cooked great Northern beans |
| ¾ | cup vegetable broth |
| ½ | tsp. dried thyme |
| ¼ | tsp. salt |
| ¼ | tsp. pepper |
| 1 | (28-oz.) can diced tomatoes, undrained |
| 1 | bay leaf |
| ¼ | cup dry breadcrumbs |
| ¼ | cup (1 ounce) shredded Parmesan cheese |
| 2 | Tbsp. butter, melted |
| 2 | links meatless Italian sausage, thawed and chopped |
| 2 | Tbsp. chopped fresh parsley |

1. Heat oil in a large nonstick skillet over medium heat. Add onion, carrot, parsnip, and garlic; cover and cook 5 minutes or until tender.

2. Place in a 5-qt. slow cooker. Add beans and next 6 ingredients. Cover and cook on LOW 8 hours or until vegetables are tender. Discard bay leaf.

3. Combine breadcrumbs, cheese, and butter in a small bowl; toss with a fork until moistened. Stir breadcrumb mixture and sausage into bean mixture; sprinkle with parsley.

**Slow-Cooker Secret:** A tagine is a Moroccan entrée cooked long and slow in a cone-shaped ceramic dish by the same name. A slow cooker perfectly duplicates the flavorful results obtained from a tagine.

# Chickpea and Vegetable Tagine

hands-on time: 3 min. • total time: 8 hr., 3 min.
makes 8 servings

| | |
|---|---|
| 2 | cups baby carrots |
| 1 | (8-oz.) container refrigerated prechopped onion |
| 1 | (14.5-oz.) can diced tomatoes with garlic |
| 2 | (15.5-oz.) cans chickpeas |
| ½ | cup sliced pitted Spanish olives |
| 2 | cups organic vegetable broth |
| 1 | tsp. ground cumin |
| ¼ | tsp. ground ginger |
| ¼ | tsp. ground turmeric |
| 1 | (3-inch) cinnamon stick |
| ½ | cup golden raisins (optional) |
| ½ | cup whole roasted, salted almonds (optional) |

Garnish: chopped fresh parsley

1. Sir together first 10 ingredients in a 4-qt. slow cooker. Cover and cook on LOW 8 to 10 hours or until vegetables are tender. Remove and discard cinnamon stick. If desired, stir in raisins, and sprinkle with almonds. Garnish, if desired.

*ideal slow cooker:*
**4-quart**

*menu idea*
for 8

Chickpea and
Vegetable Tagine

Couscous

Baklava

*groceries needed...*

Check staples: ground cumin, ground ginger, ground turmeric, cinnamon sticks

* 1 package baby carrots
* 1 (8-oz.) container refrigerated prechopped onion
* 1 (14.5-oz.) can diced tomatoes with garlic
* 2 (15.5-oz.) cans chickpeas
* 1 small can sliced pitted Spanish olives
* 1 (14-oz.) can organic vegetable broth (we tested with Swanson)
* 1 (15-oz.) package golden raisins (optional)
* 1 (6-oz.) container whole roasted, salted almonds (optional)
* 1 bunch fresh parsley (optional)

*sides...*

* 1 (10-oz.) box couscous
* Baklava from bakery

*menu idea*

**for 8 to 10**

Cheesy Grits With
Butternut Squash

Veggie sausage links

Cantaloupe wedges

*groceries needed...*

Check staples: salt, butter

- 1 (24-oz.) package regular
  yellow grits
- 1 pt. whipping cream
- 1 (32-oz.) container vegetable
  broth
- 1 (15-oz.) can butternut squash
  puree
- 1 (10¾-oz.) can Cheddar cheese
  soup
- 1 (8-oz.) package finely shredded
  sharp Cheddar cheese

*sides...*

- 2 (8-oz.) packages veggie sausage
  links
- 1 cantaloupe

**Ingredient Secret: Grits come in a variety of colors, depending on the type of corn. Feel free to use what you have on hand.**

# Cheesy Grits With Butternut Squash

hands-on time: 4 min. • total time: 4 hr., 4 min.
makes 8 to 10 servings

| | |
|---|---|
| 2 | cups uncooked regular yellow grits |
| 1 | cup whipping cream |
| 1 | tsp. salt |
| 1 | (32-oz.) container vegetable broth |
| 1 | (15-oz.) can butternut squash puree |
| 1 | (10¾-oz.) can Cheddar cheese soup |
| ¼ | cup butter, cut into 4 pieces |

**Finely shredded sharp Cheddar cheese**

**1.** Stir together first 6 ingredients in a lightly greased 4-qt. slow cooker until blended. Cover and cook on LOW 4 hours, stirring after 2 hours. Stir in butter, and sprinkle with cheese.

> **Slow-Cooker Secret:** Leaving some liquid still in the rice will make it creamier as the butter and Parmesan cheese are stirred in.

# Sweet Potato and Mushroom Risotto

hands-on time: 8 min. • total time: 2 hr., 8 min.
makes 2 to 3 servings

2   Tbsp. butter, divided
2   cups (1-inch) peeled sweet potato cubes (1 large)
½   cup refrigerated prechopped onion
¾   cup Arborio rice
½   cup dry white wine
1   (14-oz.) can vegetable broth
1   (8-oz.) package baby portobello mushrooms, quartered
2   tsp. minced fresh thyme
⅔   cup (2½ oz.) shredded Parmesan cheese
½   cup (2 oz.) shredded fontina cheese

1. Melt 1 Tbsp. butter in a large skillet over medium-high heat. Add sweet potato and onion. Cook, stirring often, 3 minutes. Add rice; cook, stirring constantly, 2 minutes. Add wine, stirring to loosen particles from bottom of skillet. Bring to a boil; remove from heat. Transfer rice mixture to a lightly greased 4-qt. slow cooker.

2. Place broth in a microwave-safe bowl. Microwave 1 minute or until hot. Stir broth, mushrooms, and thyme into rice mixture in slow cooker. Cover and cook on HIGH 2 hours or until rice is tender and liquid is almost absorbed.

3. Stir in remaining 1 Tbsp. butter and Parmesan cheese. Sprinkle with fontina cheese.

---

*ideal slow cooker:*
4-quart

*menu idea*
for 2 to 3

**Sweet Potato and Mushroom Risotto**

**Iceberg wedge with blue cheese dressing**

**Seeded flatbread**

*groceries needed...*

Check staples: butter

* 1 large sweet potato
* 1 (8-oz.) container refrigerated prechopped onion
* 1 (12-oz.) package Arborio rice
* 1 bottle dry white wine
* 1 (14-oz.) can vegetable broth
* 1 (8-oz.) package baby portobello mushrooms
* 1 bunch fresh thyme
* 1 (5-oz.) package shredded Parmesan cheese
* 1 (8-oz.) package fontina cheese

*sides...*

* 1 head iceberg lettuce
* 1 bottle blue cheese dressing
* 1 package seeded flatbread

**Slow-Cooker Secret: An oval 6- or 7-qt.
slow cooker works best for this recipe
to ensure that all the peppers can be set
in a single layer in the cooker. Place raw
peppers in the insert before beginning
the recipe to make sure there's enough
room for all to stand upright. Serve
a little of the leftover pasta sauce for
dripping the breadsticks.**

# Mushroom-Stuffed Red Peppers

hands-on time: 15 min. • total time: 4 hr., 15 min.
makes 6 servings

1   cup fire-roasted tomato and garlic pasta sauce

6   medium-size red bell peppers

4   cups coarsely chopped baby portobello mushrooms

½   cup (2 oz.) shredded Parmesan cheese, divided

⅓   cup finely chopped sweet onion

⅓   cup soft, fresh breadcrumbs

1   tsp. chopped fresh thyme

½   tsp. salt

¼   tsp. freshly ground pepper

1   (16-oz.) can navy beans, drained

1   (8.8-oz.) package precooked brown rice

Garnish: fresh thyme

**1.** Pour pasta sauce into bottom of a 7-qt. oval slow cooker.

**2.** Cut ½ inch from stem end of each bell pepper. Remove and
discard seeds and membranes.

**3.** Combine mushrooms, ¼ cup cheese, and next 7 ingredients
in a large bowl, stirring well. Spoon mushroom mixture into
bell peppers. Place peppers in a single layer in slow cooker.
Top with remaining ¼ cup cheese. Cover and cook on LOW
4 hours or until peppers are tender. Garnish, if desired.

> **Flavor Secret:** Picante sauce is a spicy sauce that is similar to salsa. It contributes a great deal of flavor in this veggie-laden dish.

# Mexican Beans and Vegetables With Rice

hands-on time: 9 min. • total time: 8 hr., 9 min.
makes 6 servings

| | |
|---|---|
| ⅔ | cup picante sauce |
| 1 | Tbsp. vegetable oil |
| 1½ | tsp. ground cumin |
| 1 | tsp. salt |
| ½ | tsp. dried oregano |
| 1 | (28-oz.) can diced tomatoes, undrained |
| 1 | (16-oz.) can red beans |
| 1 | (15-oz.) can black beans, rinsed and drained |
| 1 | large onion, chopped |
| 1 | large yellow squash or zucchini, cut into ½-inch pieces |
| 1 | green bell pepper, cut into ¾-inch pieces |
| 1 | red bell pepper, cut into ¾-inch pieces |

Hot cooked rice
Garnishes: shredded Cheddar cheese, sour cream, chopped fresh cilantro

**1.** Stir together first 12 ingredients in a 4-qt. slow cooker. Cover and cook on LOW 8 hours or until vegetables are tender. Serve over hot cooked rice. Garnish, if desired.

## ideal slow cooker:
### 4-quart

## menu idea
### for 6

**Mexican Beans and Vegetables With Rice**

**Warm flour tortillas**

**Margaritas**

## groceries needed...

Check staples: vegetable oil, ground cumin, salt, dried oregano

* 1 (16-oz.) jar picante sauce
* 1 (28-oz.) can diced tomatoes
* 1 (16-oz.) can red beans
* 1 (15-oz.) can black beans
* 1 large onion
* 1 large yellow squash or zucchini
* 1 green bell pepper
* 1 red bell pepper
* 1 (8.8-oz.) package precooked long-grain rice (such as Uncle Ben's Ready Rice)
* 1 (8-oz.) package shredded Cheddar cheese (optional)
* 1 (8-oz.) container sour cream (optional)
* 1 bunch fresh cilantro (optional)

## sides...

* 1 package 8-inch flour tortillas
* 1 bottle margarita mix
* 1 bottle tequila

*menu idea*
### for 6 to 8

Layered Mexican
Tortilla Pie

Guacamole and
tomato salad

Yellow rice

*groceries needed...*

Check staples: canola oil, chili powder, ground cumin

* 1 (8-oz.) container refrigerated prechopped onion
* 1 (12-oz.) package frozen meatless burger crumbles
* 2 (11-oz.) cans yellow corn with red and green bell peppers
* 1 (16-oz.) can refried beans
* 1 package (6-inch) flour tortillas
* 1 (18-oz.) container fresh salsa
* 1 (16-oz.) package shredded Monterey Jack cheese
* 1 (8-oz.) container sour cream
* 1 bunch fresh cilantro
* 1 (8-oz.) package shredded cheese
* 1 (12-oz.) container guacamole

*sides...*

* 1 bag shredded iceberg lettuce
* 2 tomatoes
* 2 (8-oz.) packages yellow rice

# Layered Mexican Tortilla Pie

**hands-on time: 15 min.** • **total time: 3 hr., 15 min.**
**makes 6 to 8 servings**

1     Tbsp. canola oil

½     cup refrigerated prechopped onion

1     (12-oz.) package frozen meatless burger crumbles

½     tsp. chili powder

½     tsp. ground cumin

2     (11-oz.) cans yellow corn with red and green bell peppers, drained

**Heavy-duty aluminum foil**

1     (16-oz.) can refried beans

6     (6-inch) flour tortillas

1⅔   cups fresh salsa

2¾   cups shredded Monterey Jack cheese

**Toppings: sour cream, chopped fresh cilantro, shredded Monterey Jack cheese, fresh salsa, guacamole**

**1.** Heat oil in a large nonstick skillet over medium-high heat. Add onion; cook 3 minutes or until tender. Stir in burger crumbles and next 3 ingredients. Cook 2 minutes or until crumbles are thawed. Remove from heat.

**2.** Fold 2 (17- x 12-inch) sheets of heavy-duty aluminum foil into 2 (17- x 2-inch) strips. Arrange strips in an X pattern in a lightly greased 4-qt. round slow cooker, allowing foil to extend 1 inch beyond edges of slow cooker.

**3.** Spread about ⅓ cup refried beans on 1 side of each of 5 tortillas. Place 1 tortilla, bean side up, atop foil X in slow cooker. Spoon 1 cup burger mixture over beans; top with ⅓ cup salsa and ½ cup cheese. Repeat layers 4 times. Top with remaining tortilla, and sprinkle with remaining ¼ cup cheese. Cover and cook on LOW 3 hours or until cheese melts and edges are bubbly.

**4.** Remove insert from slow cooker; let stand, uncovered, 15 minutes. Grasping ends of foil strips, carefully transfer pie to a serving plate. Carefully remove foil strips. Cut pie into wedges, and serve with desired toppings.

**Substitution Secret:** This recipe is relatively mild as is but could be spiced up with hot salsa and hot enchilada sauce. Try substituting chopped pickled jalapeños for the roasted red bell peppers for a jalapeño cornbread topping.

# Enchilada Casserole

hands-on time: 14 min. • total time: 4 hr., 19 min.
makes 6 servings

| | |
|---|---|
| 3 | Tbsp. diced green chiles, divided |
| ½ | cup mild salsa |
| ¼ | cup chopped green onions |
| ¼ | cup chopped fresh cilantro |
| 1 | (15-oz.) can black beans, drained |
| 1 | (11-oz.) can yellow corn with red and green bell peppers, drained |
| 1 | (10-oz.) can enchilada sauce |
| 2 | large eggs |
| 2 | Tbsp. chopped jarred roasted red bell peppers |
| 1 | (8.5-oz.) package corn muffin mix |
| 1½ | cups (6 oz.) shredded Mexican four-cheese blend |

Garnishes: sour cream, chopped fresh cilantro

**1.** Stir together 2 Tbsp. green chiles and next 6 ingredients in a lightly greased 4-qt. slow cooker. Cover and cook on LOW 3 hours.

**2.** Whisk eggs in a medium bowl; stir in remaining 1 Tbsp. green chiles, roasted bell peppers, and muffin mix. Spoon batter over bean mixture in slow cooker. Cover and cook on LOW 1 hour or until cornbread is done.

**3.** Sprinkle cheese over cornbread. Increase heat to HIGH; cover and cook 5 minutes or until cheese melts. Spoon into shallow bowls. Garnish, if desired.

*ideal slow cooker:*
**4-quart**

*menu idea*
**for 6**
**Enchilada Casserole**
**Green salad**

*groceries needed...*
Check staples: eggs

* 1 (7-oz.) container diced green chiles
* 1 (16-oz.) jar mild salsa
* 1 bunch green onions
* 2 bunches fresh cilantro
* 1 (15-oz.) can black beans
* 1 (11-oz.) can yellow corn with red and green bell peppers
* 1 (10-oz.) can enchilada sauce
* 1 (12-oz.) jar roasted red bell peppers
* 1 (8.5-oz.) package corn muffin mix (we tested with Jiffy)
* 1 (8-oz.) package shredded Mexican four-cheese blend
* 1 (8-oz.) container sour cream (optional)

*side...*
* Green salad from the deli

# {quick-fix desserts}

### Triple Mint Sundaes

Scoop pink peppermint, mint chocolate chip, and spearmint ice creams into julep cups or dessert glasses. Drizzle with hot fudge sauce. Garnish with a fresh mint sprig and rolled wafer cookies. Note: We tested with Pepperidge Farm Mint Chocolate Pirouette Rolled Wafers.

### Texas Float

This float is brimming with Texas flavor, and it's for the big kids. We started with some of the best vanilla ice cream this side of your grand-daddy's hand-crank freezer. Scoop ice cream into tall glasses, and top with coffee porter beer. Sprinkle with fresh raspberries. Note: We used Blue Bell Homemade Vanilla ice cream and Real Ale Shade Grown Coffee Porter, but you can substitute another Texas brew, Shiner Bohemian Black Lager.

## Strawberries With a Chocolate Accent

**M**elt chocolate in the microwave in 30-second intervals, stirring between each, give strawberries a quick dip, and then add a Southern touch by rolling them in chopped pecans.

# soups and stews

Nothing soothes the soul more than a bowlful of a hearty soup or stew. ✹ Surefire pleasers like Easy Brunswick Stew, Three-Cheese Broccoli Soup, and Chicken and Rice Soup With Mushrooms come together quickly for a delicious dinner. ✹ Always satisfying, these soups and stews simmer all day and have been perfected for fast preparation and incredible flavor.

*ideal slow cooker:*
5-quart

# Corn and Potato Chowder

hands-on time: 15 min. • total time: 8 hr., 15 min.
makes 4 to 6 servings

| | |
|---|---|
| 1 | lb. baking potatoes, peeled and cut into ¼-inch cubes (about 2 cups) |
| 1 | (14.75-oz.) can cream-style corn |
| 1 | (14.5-oz.) can diced tomatoes |
| 1 | (14-oz.) can chicken broth |
| ½ | cup chopped onion |
| ½ | cup coarsely chopped celery |
| ¾ | tsp. dried basil |
| ½ | tsp. salt |
| ¼ | tsp. pepper |
| 1 | bay leaf |
| 1 | cup whipping cream |
| ¼ | cup butter |
| 4 | bacon slices, cooked and crumbled |

Chopped green onions

1. Stir together first 10 ingredients in a 5-qt. slow cooker. Cover and cook on LOW 8 hours or until potato is tender. Add whipping cream and butter, stirring until butter melts. Discard bay leaf. Ladle into bowls; sprinkle each serving with bacon and chopped green onions.

*menu idea*
### for 4 to 6

**Corn and Potato Chowder**

**Baked snack crackers**

*groceries needed...*

Check staples: dried basil, salt, pepper, butter, bay leaves

* 1 lb. baking potatoes
* 1 (14.75-oz.) can cream-style corn
* 1 (14.5-oz.) can diced tomatoes
* 1 (14-oz.) can chicken broth
* 1 onion
* 1 bunch celery
* 1 pt. whipping cream
* 1 package bacon
* 1 bunch green onions

*side...*

* 1 (10-oz.) package baked snack crackers

menu idea
for 6 to 8

**Parsnip and Pear Soup**

**Grilled ham and cheese sandwiches**

groceries needed...

Check staples: olive oil, salt, pepper, mayonnaise

* 1 (8-oz.) container refrigerated prechopped onion
* 1 garlic bulb
* 1 (32-oz.) container chicken broth
* 1 bunch fresh rosemary
* 2 lb. parsnips
* 2 ripe pears
* 1 pt. half-and-half
* 1 package cooked bacon (optional)

side...

* 1 loaf sandwich bread
* 1 to 1½ lb. deli-sliced ham
* ½ lb. sliced Swiss cheese

**Ingredient Secret:** A parsnip is a creamy-white, carrot-shaped root vegetable with a unique piquant, yet sweet flavor. Avoid parsnips that are limp or have brown spots.

# Parsnip and Pear Soup

hands-on time: 15 min. • total time: 7 hr., 15 min.
makes 6 to 8 servings

| | |
|---|---|
| 1 | Tbsp. olive oil |
| ½ | cup refrigerated prechopped onion |
| 4 | garlic cloves, minced |
| 5 | cups chicken broth |
| 2 | tsp. chopped fresh rosemary |
| ½ | tsp. salt |
| ½ | tsp. freshly ground pepper |
| 2 | lb. parsnips, peeled and chopped |
| 2 | ripe pears, peeled and chopped |
| ½ | cup half-and-half |

Garnishes: cooked and crumbled bacon, fresh rosemary sprigs

**1.** Heat oil in a large skillet over medium-high heat. Add onion and garlic; sauté 3 minutes or until tender.

**2.** Combine onion mixture, broth, and next 5 ingredients in a 4-qt. slow cooker. Cover and cook on HIGH for 7 hours.

**3.** Stir half-and-half into soup. Process soup, in batches, in a blender until smooth, stopping to scrape down sides as necessary. Pour soup into bowls. Garnish, if desired.

**Slow-Cooker Secret:** Stirring the cheese cubes into the soup first helps the other cheeses melt smoother when they're added.

*ideal slow cooker:*
4-quart

# Three-Cheese Broccoli Soup

hands-on time: 15 min. • total time: 4 hr., 15 min.
makes 8 servings

¼  cup butter

1  large onion, chopped

¼  cup all-purpose flour

1  (12-oz.) can evaporated milk

1  (32-oz.) container chicken broth

¼  tsp. salt

½  tsp. freshly ground pepper

1  (14-oz.) package frozen baby broccoli florets

1  (8-oz.) package pasteurized prepared cheese product, cubed

1½  cups (6 oz.) shredded extra-sharp Cheddar cheese

1  cup shredded Parmesan cheese

Garnish: shredded extra-sharp Cheddar cheese

1. Melt butter in a large skillet over medium-high heat. Add onion. Sauté 4 minutes or until tender. Stir in flour. Cook, stirring constantly, 1 minute. Gradually stir in milk until smooth. Pour milk mixture into a lightly greased 4-qt. slow cooker. Stir in broth and next 3 ingredients. Cover and cook on LOW 4 hours or until bubbly.

2. Add cheese cubes, stirring until cubes melt. Add Cheddar cheese and Parmesan cheese, stirring until cheeses melt. Garnish, if desired. Serve immediately.

*menu idea*
for 8

**Three-Cheese Broccoli Soup**

**Crusty rustic bread**

**Fresh fruit**

*groceries needed...*

Check staples: butter, flour, salt, pepper

* 1 large onion
* 1 (12-oz.) can evaporated milk
* 1 (32-oz.) container chicken broth
* 1 (14-oz.) package frozen baby broccoli florets
* 1 (8-oz.) package pasteurized prepared cheese product
* 1 (8-oz.) package extra-sharp Cheddar cheese
* 1 (5-oz.) package shredded Parmesan cheese

*sides...*

* 1 loaf crusty rustic bread
* Assorted fresh fruit

# Beer and Sharp Cheddar Soup With Baguette Toasts

hands-on time: 6 min. • total time: 2 hr., 51 min.
makes 6 servings

*menu idea*
### for 6

**Beer and
Sharp Cheddar Soup
With Baguette Toasts**

**Romaine salad**

*groceries needed...*

Check staples: butter, jarred minced garlic, flour, salt, pepper, Worcestershire sauce (optional), paprika (optional), salad dressing

* 1 (8-oz.) container refrigerated prechopped celery, onion, and bell pepper mix
* 1 bunch carrots
* 1 pt. half-and-half
* 1 (14-oz.) can chicken broth
* 1 (12-oz.) package shredded sharp Cheddar cheese
* 1 (12-oz.) can beer
* 1 French bread baguette
* 1 can olive oil cooking spray
* 1 bulb fresh garlic (optional)

*side...*

* 1 head romaine lettuce
* 1 pt. grape tomatoes

| | |
|---|---|
| ⅓ | cup butter |
| 1½ | cups refrigerated prechopped celery, onion, and bell pepper mix |
| 2 | carrots, chopped |
| 1 | Tbsp. jarred minced garlic |
| ½ | cup all-purpose flour |
| 2 | cups half-and-half |
| 1 | cup chicken broth |
| 3 | cups (12 oz.) shredded sharp Cheddar cheese |
| 1 | (12-oz.) can beer |

Salt and pepper to taste

| | |
|---|---|
| 1 | Tbsp. Worcestershire sauce (optional) |
| ½ | (8.5-oz.) French bread baguette |
| 1 | bulb fresh garlic (optional) |

Paprika (optional)

Olive oil cooking spray

**1.** Melt butter in a large saucepan over medium-high heat. Add celery mixture, carrot, and garlic; sauté 5 to 6 minutes or just until tender. Whisk in flour until smooth. Cook 1 minute, stirring constantly. Gradually whisk in half-and-half and broth; cook over medium heat, whisking constantly, 3 to 4 minutes or until thickened and bubbly. Transfer to a 4-qt. slow cooker. Stir in cheese and beer. Cover and cook on LOW 2½ hours. Season to taste with salt and pepper. Add Worcestershire sauce, if desired.

**2.** Preheat oven to 450°. Cut baguette diagonally into ½-inch slices. Rub baguette slices with cut garlic cloves, if desired. Dust slices with paprika, if desired. Arrange baguette slices on a baking sheet; coat with cooking spray. Bake at 450° for 3 to 4 minutes or until toasted. Serve baguette toasts with soup.

# Loaded Potato Soup

hands-on time: 15 min. • total time: 8 hr., 35 min.
makes 8 servings

4   lb. new potatoes, peeled and cut into ¼-inch-thick slices
1   small onion, chopped
2   (14-oz.) cans chicken broth
2   tsp. salt
½   tsp. pepper
2   cups half-and-half
Toppings: shredded Cheddar cheese, cooked and crumbled bacon, sliced green onions

1. Layer sliced potatoes in a lightly greased 5-qt. slow cooker; top with chopped onion.

2. Stir together chicken broth, salt, and pepper; pour over potatoes and onion. (Broth will not completely cover potatoes and onion.) Cover and cook on LOW 8 hours or until potatoes are tender. Mash mixture with a potato masher; stir in half-and-half. Cover and cook on HIGH 20 more minutes or until mixture is thoroughly heated. Ladle into bowls, and serve with desired toppings.

*ideal slow cooker:*
5-quart

*menu idea*
for 8
**Loaded Potato Soup**
**Lettuce wedges with Ranch dressing**
**Soft breadsticks**

*groceries needed...*
Check staples: salt, pepper
* 4 lb. new potatoes
* 1 small onion
* 2 (14-oz.) cans chicken broth
* 1 pt. half-and-half
* 1 (8-oz.) package shredded Cheddar cheese
* 1 package bacon
* 1 bunch green onions

*sides...*
* 1 head iceberg lettuce
* 1 bottle Ranch dressing
* 1 package soft breaksticks

**groceries needed...**

Check staples: butter, salt, pepper, salad dressing

* 6 large sweet onions
* 1 (32-oz.) container beef broth
* 2 (10½-oz.) cans beef consommé
* 1 bottle dry white wine
* 1 bunch fresh thyme leaves
* 1 French bread baguette
* 1 package shredded Gruyère cheese

**side...**

* 2 or 3 bags mixed salad greens

Make-Ahead Secret: This soup makes a large volume and freezes well if not eaten all at once.

# French Onion Soup

hands-on time: 8 min. • total time: 8 hr., 23 min.
makes 8 to 10 servings

| 6 | large sweet onions, thinly sliced |
| ¼ | cup butter, melted |
| ½ | tsp. salt |
| ½ | tsp. freshly ground pepper |
| 1 | (32-oz.) container beef broth |
| 2 | (10½-oz.) cans beef consommé |
| ¼ | cup dry white wine |
| 1 | tsp. fresh thyme leaves |
| 8 | to 10 (½-inch-thick) French bread baguette slices |
| ½ | cup (2 ounces) shredded Gruyère cheese |

Garnish: fresh thyme

1. Combine first 4 ingredients in a lightly greased 5- to 6-qt. slow cooker. Cover and cook on LOW 8 hours.

2. Stir broth and next 3 ingredients into onion mixture. Cover and cook 15 more minutes or until hot.

3. Meanwhile, preheat broiler with oven rack 3 inches from heat. Sprinkle baguette slices with shredded cheese; place on a lightly greased baking sheet. Broil 1 to 2 minutes or until cheese melts. Serve soup with cheese toasts. Garnish, if desired.

**Slow-Cooker Secret:** We used an immersion blender to easily puree the soup right in the slow cooker. If you don't have one, puree the soup, in batches, in a food processor or blender after allowing soup to cool 20 minutes.

*ideal slow cooker:*
5-quart

*menu idea*
for 6

**Butternut Squash Soup With Vanilla Bean**

**Gourmet grilled cheese sandwich**

# Butternut Squash Soup With Vanilla Bean

hands-on time: 8 min. • total time: 6 hr., 28 min.
makes 6 servings

3   (11-oz.) containers refrigerated cubed peeled butternut squash (6 cups), chopped
1   cup refrigerated prechopped onion
1   Braeburn apple, peeled and coarsely chopped
1½  cups apple cider
1   cup chicken broth
1   vanilla bean, split lengthwise
1   rosemary sprig
½   cup whipping cream
¼   tsp. salt
Garnishes: fresh rosemary, additional whipping cream

**1.** Stir together first 5 ingredients in a 5-qt. slow cooker. Scrape vanilla bean seeds into slow cooker; add vanilla bean pod and rosemary sprig. Stir well. Cover and cook on LOW 6 hours or until squash is very tender. Uncover and cool 20 minutes. Discard vanilla bean and rosemary.

**2.** Process mixture with a handheld blender (immersion blender) until smooth. Stir in whipping cream and salt. Garnish, if desired.

*groceries needed...*

Check staples: salt, butter

* 3 (11-oz.) containers refrigerated cubed peeled butternut squash
* 1 (8-oz.) container refrigerated prechopped onion
* 1 Braeburn apple
* 1 bottle apple cider
* 1 (14-oz.) can chicken broth
* 1 bottle vanilla beans
* 1 bunch rosemary
* 1 pt. whipping cream

*side...*

* 1 loaf Chicago Italian bread
* 1 (8-oz.) package sliced Cheddar cheese

*menu idea*
### for 6 to 8

Roasted Mushroom
Soup With Sourdough
Croutons

Garden salad

White wine

*groceries needed...*

Check staples: olive oil, kosher salt, pepper, jarred minced garlic, ground sage, ground nutmeg, flour, salad dressing

* 4 (4-oz.) packages sliced fresh gourmet mushroom blend
* 2 (8-oz.) packages sliced fresh mushrooms
* 2 (8-oz.) containers refrigerated prechopped celery, onion, and bell pepper mix
* 1 bottle dry white wine
* 2 (14-oz.) cans vegetable broth
* 1 pt. heavy cream
* 1 loaf sourdough bread
* 1 bunch fresh chives

*side...*

* 2 or 3 (5-oz.) packages fresh baby garden salad blend

# Roasted Mushroom Soup With Sourdough Croutons

hands-on time: 15 min. • total time: 3 hr., 27 min.
makes 6 to 8 servings

| | |
|---|---|
| 4 | (4-oz.) packages sliced fresh gourmet mushroom blend |
| 2 | (8-oz.) packages sliced fresh mushrooms |
| 4 | Tbsp. olive oil, divided |
| 1 | tsp. kosher salt |
| $\frac{1}{2}$ | tsp. freshly ground pepper |
| 2 | (8-oz.) containers refrigerated prechopped celery, onion, and bell pepper mix |
| 1 | Tbsp. jarred minced garlic |
| 1 | cup dry white wine |
| 2 | cups vegetable broth |
| $\frac{1}{2}$ | tsp. ground sage |
| $\frac{1}{4}$ | tsp. ground nutmeg |
| 1 | cup heavy cream |
| $\frac{1}{4}$ | cup all-purpose flour |
| 4 | (1-inch-thick) sourdough bread slices, cut into 1-inch cubes |

Garnish: chopped fresh chives

**1.** Preheat broiler with oven rack $5\frac{1}{2}$ inches from heat. Spread mushrooms in a single layer on an aluminum foil-lined rimmed baking sheet. Drizzle with 2 Tbsp. olive oil; sprinkle with salt and pepper. Broil 12 minutes or until browned. Heat 1 Tbsp. oil in a skillet over medium-high heat. Add celery mixture and garlic; sauté 3 minutes. Stir in wine, and cook 5 minutes or until reduced by half.

**2.** Combine mushrooms and juices, onion mixture, broth, and next 2 ingredients in a 5-qt. slow cooker. Cover and cook on HIGH 3 hours. Stir cream into soup. Stir together flour and $\frac{1}{4}$ cup water until smooth. Stir into soup. Cover and cook 15 more minutes or until thickened. During last 30 minutes of cook time, preheat oven to 350°. Toss bread cubes with remaining 1 Tbsp. oil. Place on a baking sheet. Bake at 350° for 10 minutes. Garnish, if desired.

ideal slow cooker:
### 5- to 6-quart

# Potlikker Soup

hands-on time: 10 min.  •  total time: 6 hr., 10 min.
makes 6 to 8 servings

1   Tbsp. olive oil
2   cups refrigerated prechopped onion
½   cup chopped carrot
2   garlic cloves, minced
1   (1-lb.) ham hock
4   (1-lb.) packages fresh collard greens, cleaned, trimmed, and chopped
½   teaspoon salt
½   teaspoon freshly ground pepper
¼   teaspoon crushed red pepper
1   (32-oz.) container chicken broth

1. Heat oil in a large skillet over medium-high heat; add onion and carrot, and sauté 4 minutes or until tender. Add garlic; sauté 1 minute. Place vegetables, 4 cups water, ham hock, and remaining ingredients in a 5- to 6-qt. slow cooker. Cover and cook on HIGH 1 hour. Reduce heat to LOW and cook 5 hours or until ham falls off the bone. Remove ham hock from slow cooker. Remove ham from bone, discarding bone. Chop ham, and stir into soup.

*menu idea*
### for 6 to 8

Potlikker Soup
Cornbread muffins

*groceries needed...*

Check staples: olive oil, salt, pepper, crushed red pepper

❋ 2 (8-oz.) containers refrigerated prechopped onion
❋ 1 bunch carrots
❋ 1 garlic bulb
❋ 1 (1-lb.) ham hock
❋ 4 (1 lb.) packages fresh collard greens
❋ 1 (32-oz.) container chicken broth

*side...*

❋ 1 (8.5-oz.) package corn muffin mix

*groceries needed...*

Check staples: ground turmeric, ground ginger, salt, pepper, ground cinnamon

- 1 (16-oz.) package dried lentils
- 1 (11-oz.) container refrigerated cubed peeled butternut squash
- 1 bunch carrots
- 1 (0.02-oz.) jar saffron threads
- 2 (14.5-ounce) cans diced tomatoes
- 1 large onion
- 1 garlic bulb

*side...*

- 1 package flatbread

**Ingredient Secret:** Look for cubed peeled butternut squash in the produce section of your supermarket. It's one of the keys to making the prep for this recipe a snap. However, if you start with a whole squash, pierce it several times with a paring knife, and microwave it at HIGH for 1 minute. This will make it easier to peel. Cut squash in half, scrape out the seeds, then cut it into cubes.

## Moroccan Lentil Stew

hands-on time: 11 min. • total time: 8 hr., 11 min.
makes 8 servings

| | |
|---|---|
| 1 | cup dried lentils |
| 2 | cups refrigerated cubed peeled butternut squash |
| 1 | cup sliced carrot |
| 2 | tsp. ground turmeric |
| 1 | tsp. ground ginger |
| ¼ | tsp. salt |
| ½ | tsp. freshly ground pepper |
| ½ | tsp. ground cinnamon |

Pinch of saffron threads

| | |
|---|---|
| 2 | (14.5-oz.) cans diced tomatoes, undrained |
| 1 | large onion, chopped |
| 3 | garlic cloves, minced |

1. Rinse and sort lentils according to package directions. Stir together lentils, squash, 2 cups water, and next 10 ingredients in a 5-qt. slow cooker. Cover and cook on LOW 8 hours.

# Vegetable Tortellini Soup

**hands-on time: 5 min.** • **total time: 7 hr., 23 minutes**
**makes 6 servings**

2 (8-oz.) packages refrigerated prechopped celery, onion, and bell pepper mix

½ tsp. pepper

1 medium zucchini, coarsely chopped

1 (32-oz.) container chicken broth

1 (16-oz.) package frozen baby corn, bean, pea, and carrot mix

1 (15.5-oz) can cannellini beans, drained

1 (14.5-oz.) can diced tomatoes with basil, oregano, and garlic, undrained

1 (9-oz.) package refrigerated cheese tortellini

**Garnish: shredded Parmesan cheese**

1. Heat a large nonstick skillet over medium-high heat. Coat pan with cooking spray. Add celery mixture, and sauté 5 minutes or until tender. Transfer mixture to a 5-qt. slow cooker. Stir in pepper and next 5 ingredients. Cover and cook on LOW for 7 hours.

2. Increase heat to HIGH; add tortellini. Cover and cook 18 minutes or until pasta is tender. Garnish, if desired.

## ideal slow cooker:
### 5-quart

## menu idea
### for 6

Vegetable Tortellini Soup

Whole wheat French bread

## groceries needed...

Check staples: pepper

- 2 (8-oz.) containers refrigerated prechopped celery, onion, and bell pepper mix
- 1 medium zucchini
- 1 (32-oz.) container chicken broth
- 1 (16-oz.) package frozen baby corn, bean, pea, and carrot mix (we tested with Birds Eye)
- 1 (15.5-oz) can cannellini beans
- 1 (14.5-oz.) can diced tomatoes with basil, oregano, and garlic
- 1 (9-oz.) package refrigerated cheese tortellini
- 1 (5-oz.) package shredded Parmesan cheese (optional)

## side...

- 1 loaf whole wheat French bread

*menu idea*

for 6 to 8

**Black-eyed Pea Soup**

**Coleslaw**

**Cornbread**

*groceries needed...*

Check staples: jarred minced garlic

* 1 (16-oz.) package dried black-eyed peas
* 1 package bacon
* 1 (8-oz.) container refrigerated prechopped onion
* 1 medium-size red bell pepper
* 1 (48-oz.) container chicken broth
* 1 (14.5-oz.) can diced tomatoes and zesty mild green chiles (we tested with Del Monte)
* 1 bunch green onions (optional)

*sides...*

* 2 pt. deli coleslaw
* 1 package corrnbread mix

**Slow-Cooker Secret: If you have the up-front time, you can use the following method to soak the peas for this soup. Place peas in a Dutch oven; add water 2 inches above peas. Bring to a boil. Boil 1 minute; cover, remove from heat, and let stand 1 hour. Drain. Proceed as directed in recipe.**

# Black-eyed Pea Soup

hands-on time: 11 min. • total time: 20 hr., 11 min.
makes 6 to 8 servings

1   (16-oz.) package dried black-eyed peas
6   bacon slices
1   (8-oz.) container refrigerated prechopped onion
1   medium-size red bell pepper, chopped
1   (48-oz.) container chicken broth
1   Tbsp. jarred minced garlic
1   (14.5-oz.) can diced tomatoes and zesty mild green chiles, undrained

Garnish: chopped green onions

1. Rinse and sort peas according to package directions. Place peas in a Dutch oven. Cover with water 2 inches above peas; let soak 8 hours. Drain. Place peas in a 6-qt. slow cooker.

2. Cook bacon in a large skillet over medium-high heat 5 to 7 minutes or until crisp; remove bacon, and drain on paper towels, reserving drippings in skillet. Coarsely crumble bacon.

3. Add onion to drippings in skillet; cook, stirring constantly, 4 minutes or until tender. Stir bacon, onion, bell pepper, and next 3 ingredients into peas in slow cooker. Cover and cook on LOW 12 hours or until peas are tender. Garnish, if desired.

# 15-Bean and Tomato Soup

hands-on time: 14 min. • total time: 18 hr., 14 min.
makes 12 servings

1  (20-oz.) package 15-bean soup mix
4  bacon slices
2  cups refrigerated prechopped onion
½  cup chopped carrot (about 1 small)
2  garlic cloves, pressed
½  tsp. chopped fresh rosemary
¼  tsp. salt
¼  tsp. freshly ground pepper
2  (32-oz.) containers chicken broth
2  (14.5-oz.) cans diced tomatoes with balsamic vinegar, basil, and oil, undrained

Garnishes: shaved Parmesan, fresh rosemary

1. Rinse and sort bean mix according to package directions. Place bean mix in a 6-qt. slow cooker, reserving seasoning packet for another use. Cover with water 2 inches above bean mix; let soak 8 hours. Drain and return to slow cooker.

2. Cook bacon in a large skillet over medium-high heat 5 to 7 minutes or until crisp. Remove bacon, and drain on paper towels; reserve drippings in skillet. Crumble bacon. Sauté onion and carrot in hot drippings 3 minutes or until tender. Add garlic; sauté 1 minute.

3. Stir bacon, vegetable mixture, rosemary, and remaining ingredients into bean mix in slow cooker. Cover and cook on LOW 10 hours or until beans are tender. Garnish, if desired.

*menu idea*

**for 8**

Chicken and
Rice Soup
With Mushrooms

**Herbed breadsticks**

*groceries needed...*

Check staples: olive oil

✳ 1 (8-oz.) container refrigerated prechopped onion

✳ 1 (8-oz.) container refrigerated prechopped celery

✳ 1 (8-oz.) package sliced fresh mushrooms

✳ 1 garlic bulb

✳ 1 (32-oz.) container plus 1 (14-oz.) can chicken broth

✳ 1 rotisserie chicken

✳ 1 bundle fresh parsley

✳ 1 (4-oz.) jar chicken bouillon granules

✳ 1 (6-oz.) package long-grain and wild rice mix (we tested with Uncle Ben's)

*side...*

✳ 1 (11-oz.) container refrigerated breadsticks

✳ Fresh or dried herbs

**Ingredient Secret: For convenience, use a rotisserie chicken in this soup. The average rotisserie chicken will yield about 3 cups of chopped cooked chicken.**

# Chicken and Rice Soup With Mushrooms

hands-on time: 10 min. • total time: 4 hr., 40 min.
makes 8 servings

1   Tbsp. olive oil

1   cup refrigerated prechopped onion

½   cup refrigerated prechopped celery

1   (8-oz.) package sliced fresh mushrooms

2   garlic cloves, minced

5   cups chicken broth

3   cups chopped cooked chicken

2   Tbsp. chopped fresh parsley

1   tsp. chicken bouillon granules

1   (6-oz.) package long-grain and wild rice mix

**1.** Heat a large skillet over medium-high heat; add oil. Add onion and next 3 ingredients. Sauté 4 minutes or until vegetables are tender; add 2 cups water, stirring to loosen particles from bottom of skillet. Combine vegetable mixture, broth, and remaining ingredients (including seasoning packet from rice mix) in a 4- to 5-qt. slow cooker. Cover and cook on LOW 4 to 4½ hours or until rice is tender.

**Ingredient Secret:** We used flavorful smoked chicken from a local barbecue restaurant for this recipe. Your grocery store may carry smoked chicken. Just be sure to ask for it without sauce.

*ideal slow cooker:*
5-quart

# Smoked Chicken-Banana Pepper Soup

hands-on time: 12 min. • total time: 6 hr., 22 min.
makes 8 servings

*menu idea*
for 8
**Smoked Chicken-Banana Pepper Soup**
**Limeade**

4   bacon slices
1   (8-oz.) container refrigerated prechopped celery, onion, and bell pepper mix
6   cups low-sodium fat-free chicken broth
2   cups sliced pickled banana peppers
2   Tbsp. juice from banana peppers
1   tsp. ground cumin
½   tsp. dried oregano
½   tsp. salt
½   tsp. pepper
8   plum tomatoes, chopped
1   lb. pulled smoked chicken
1   (14-oz.) package boil-in-bag white rice
Garnish: fresh oregano

*groceries needed...*

Check staples: ground cumin, dried oregano, salt, pepper

✳ 1 package bacon
✳ 1 (8-oz.) container refrigerated prechopped celery, onion, and bell pepper mix
✳ 1 (32-oz.) container low-sodium fat-free chicken broth
✳ 1 (16-oz.) jar sliced pickled banana peppers
✳ 8 plum tomatoes
✳ 1 lb. pulled smoked chicken
✳ 1 (14-oz.) package boil-in-bag white rice
✳ 1 bunch fresh oregano (optional)

*side...*
✳ 1 (12-oz.) can frozen limeade concentrate, thawed

1. Cook bacon in a large skillet over medium-high heat 5 to 7 minutes or until crisp; remove bacon, and drain on paper towels, reserving drippings in skillet. Coarsely crumble bacon.

2. Add celery mixture to drippings in skillet; cook, stirring constantly, 5 minutes or until tender. Add chicken broth, stirring to loosen particles from bottom of skillet. Transfer broth mixture to a 5-qt. slow cooker. Stir in bacon, peppers, and next 7 ingredients. Cover and cook on LOW for 6 hours. Stir in rice. Cover and cook 10 minutes or until rice is tender. Garnish, if desired.

*ideal slow cooker:*

**6-quart**

*menu idea*

**for 6**

Slow-Cooker
Beer-Braised Pork
and Black Bean Soup

Cornbread
crackers

*groceries needed...*

Check staples: olive oil, ground cumin,
kosher salt

* 1½ lb. boneless pork shoulder
  roast (Boston butt)
* 2 (12-oz.) bottles beer
* 1 (12-oz.) can chipotle peppers
  in adobo sauce
* 1 large onion
* 1 lb. dried black beans
* 1 (8-oz.) container sour cream
* 1 (18-oz.) container store-bought
  refrigerated fresh salsa
* 1 bunch fresh cilantro

*side...*

* 1 (12-oz.) package cornbread
  crackers

**Slow-Cooker Secret:** Browning the roast before slow cooking develops extra flavor and color. A slow cooker that has an insert that can go from stovetop to the cooker is ideal for this recipe.

# Slow-Cooker Beer-Braised Pork and Black Bean Soup

hands-on time: 11 min. • total time: 8 hr., 11 min.
makes 6 servings

1½ lb. boneless pork shoulder roast (Boston butt)

2 Tbsp. olive oil

2 (12-oz.) bottles beer

1 Tbsp. chopped canned chipotle peppers in adobo sauce
plus 1 Tbsp. adobo sauce

1 tsp. ground cumin

1 large onion, chopped

1 lb. dried black beans, rinsed

1½ tsp. kosher salt

½ cup sour cream

½ cup store-bought refrigerated fresh salsa

¼ cup chopped fresh cilantro

1. Cook pork in hot olive oil in a Dutch oven over medium-high heat 3 minutes on each side or until browned on all sides.

2. Combine beer, 3 cups water, peppers, adobo sauce, cumin, onion, beans, pork, and 1½ tsp. salt in a 6-qt. slow cooker. Cover and cook on LOW 8 hours. Using a fork, separate pork into large pieces. Divide among individual bowls, and top with sour cream, salsa, and cilantro.

**Slow-Cooker Secret: Sirloin tip is a leaner cut than traditional chuck roast. It yields a very tender "fall-apart" texture after the long, slow cooking.**

*ideal slow cooker:*
4-quart

# Steak Soup

hands-on time: 15 min. • total time: 8 hr., 45 min.
makes 6 servings

2¼ lb. sirloin tip roast, cut into 1-inch cubes

¼ cup all-purpose flour

½ tsp. salt

½ tsp. coarsely ground pepper

2 Tbsp. canola oil

1 (1-oz.) envelope dry onion soup mix

4 cups beef broth

1 Tbsp. tomato paste

1 Tbsp. Worcestershire sauce

2 cups uncooked wide egg noodles

**1.** Combine first 4 ingredients in a large zip-top plastic freezer bag; seal bag, and shake to coat beef.

**2.** Sauté beef in hot oil in a Dutch oven over medium-high heat 6 minutes or until browned. Place in a 4-qt. slow cooker. Sprinkle onion soup mix over beef. Whisk together beef broth, tomato paste, and Worcestershire; pour over beef. Cover and cook on LOW 8 hours or until beef is tender.

**3.** Add noodles to slow cooker; cover and cook 30 minutes or until noodles are done.

*menu idea*
for 6

**Steak Soup**

**Caesar salad**

**Cheese garlic mini-muffins**

*groceries needed...*

Check staples: flour, salt, coarsely ground pepper, canola oil, Worcestershire sauce

❋ 2¼ lb. sirloin tip roast

❋ 1 box dry onion soup mix

❋ 1 (32-oz.) container beef broth

❋ 1 (6-oz.) can tomato paste

❋ 1 (12-oz.) package wide egg noodles

*sides...*

❋ 2 (9.9-oz.) packages Caesar salad kit

❋ Bakery muffins or boxed muffin mix

*groceries needed...*

Check staples: flour, canola oil,
jarred minced garlic, balsamic vinegar,
Worcestershire sauce, pepper,
bay leaves, salt

- 1 (4-lb.) sirloin tip beef roast
- 1 (8-oz) container refrigerated
  prechopped red onion
- 2 large baking potatoes
- 1 (16-oz.) package baby carrots
- 2 (12-oz.) bottles lager beer*
- 1 (.25-oz.) jar dried parsley flakes
- 1 (4-oz.) jar beef bouillon granules

*side...*

- 1 (8.5-oz.) French bread baguette

# Peppered Beef Soup

hands-on time: 13 min.  •  total time: 7 hr., 13 min.
makes 6 servings

| | |
|---|---|
| 1 | (4-lb.) sirloin tip beef roast |
| ½ | cup all-purpose flour |
| 2 | Tbsp. canola oil |
| 1 | cup refrigerated prechopped red onion |
| 2 | tsp. jarred minced garlic |
| 2 | large baking potatoes, peeled and diced |
| 1 | (16-oz.) package baby carrots |
| 2 | (12-oz.) bottles lager beer* |
| 2 | Tbsp. balsamic vinegar |
| 2 | Tbsp. Worcestershire sauce |
| 2 | Tbsp. dried parsley flakes |
| 1 | Tbsp. beef bouillon granules |
| 1½ | to 3 tsp. freshly ground pepper |
| 4 | bay leaves |
| ½ | tsp. salt |

**1.** Rinse roast, and pat dry. Cut a 1-inch-deep cavity in the shape of an "X" on top of roast. (Do not cut all the way through roast.) Dredge roast in flour; shake off excess.

**2.** Cook roast in hot oil in a Dutch oven over medium-high heat 1 to 2 minutes on each side or until lightly browned.

**3.** Place roast in a 6-qt. slow cooker. Stuff cavity with sliced red onion and minced garlic; top roast with potatoes and baby carrots. Pour beer, balsamic vinegar, and Worcestershire sauce into slow cooker. Sprinkle with parsley, bouillon, and ground pepper. Add bay leaves to liquid in slow cooker.

**4.** Cover and cook on LOW 7 to 8 hours or until fork-tender. Shred roast using two forks. Season with salt. Discard bay leaves.

*3 cups low-sodium beef broth may be substituted.

**Slow-Cooker Secret:** Don't be tempted to add more liquid because as the vegetables cook, they release enough liquid to make this thick stew the right consistency.

# Smokehouse Chicken and Vegetable Stew

hands-on time: 5 min. • total time: 8 hr., 5 min.
makes 8 servings

1    cup chicken broth

½    cup sweet and spicy barbecue sauce

1¼   cups refrigerated prechopped tricolor bell pepper

1    cup frozen baby lima beans

2    Tbsp. Worcestershire sauce

½    tsp. salt

½    tsp. pepper

2    lb. pulled smoked chicken

1    (26-oz.) jar fire-roasted tomato and garlic pasta sauce

1    (16-oz.) package frozen mixed vegetables

1    (8-oz.) container refrigerated prechopped onion

1. Combine all ingredients in a 5-qt. slow cooker. Cover and cook on HIGH 8 hours.

*groceries needed...*

Check staples: Worcestershire sauce, salt, pepper

* 1 (14-oz.) can chicken broth
* 1 (18-oz.) bottle sweet and spicy barbecue sauce (we tested with Sweet Baby Ray's)
* 1 (8-oz.) container refrigerated prechopped tricolor bell pepper
* 1 (12-oz.) package frozen baby lima beans
* 2 lb. pulled smoked chicken
* 1 (26-oz) jar fire-roasted tomato and garlic pasta sauce (we tested with Classico)
* 1 (16-oz.) package frozen mixed vegetables
* 1 (8-oz.) container refrigerated prechopped onion

*side...*

* Deli cornbread or boxed cornbread mix

*groceries needed...*

Check staples: olive oil, jarred minced garlic, kosher salt, ground cumin, chili powder, pepper

* 2 skinned and boned chicken breasts (about 1 lb.)
* 4 skinned and boned chicken thighs (about 10.5 oz.)
* 2 baking potatoes (about 1½ lb.)
* 1 (10-oz.) package frozen sweet corn
* 1 bunch celery
* 1 bunch carrots
* 1 onion
* 1 (12.5 oz.) jar salsa
* 2 (14-oz.) cans chicken broth
* 1 package (6-inch) corn tortillas

*side...*

* 1 package chocolate chip cookies

**Ingredient Secret:** If you know that you will be using chopped vegetables in meals like this one several times during the week, chop them all at once and then store them in zip-top plastic bags.

# Spicy Chicken Stew

hands-on time: 15 min.  •  total time: 6 hr., 15 min.
makes 6 servings

| | |
|---|---|
| 2 | skinned and boned chicken breasts (about 1 lb.) |
| 4 | skinned and boned chicken thighs (about 10.5 oz.) |
| 1 | Tbsp. olive oil |
| 2 | baking potatoes (about 1½ lb.), peeled and cut into chunks (3⅓ cups) |
| 2 | cups frozen sweet corn |
| 2 | stalks celery, chopped |
| 2 | carrots, peeled and cut into chunks (1 cup) |
| 1 | onion, thickly sliced |
| 1 | tsp. jarred minced garlic |
| 1 | (12.5 oz.) jar salsa |
| 2 | tsp. kosher salt |
| 1½ | tsp. ground cumin |
| 1 | tsp. chili powder |
| ½ | tsp. pepper |
| 2½ | cups chicken broth |
| 4 | (6-inch) corn tortillas, cut into strips |

**1.** Cook chicken in hot olive oil in a Dutch oven over medium-high heat 3 minutes on each side or until browned.

**2.** Place potatoes, corn, celery, carrots, onion, and garlic in a 5-qt. slow cooker. Stir in salsa, salt, cumin, chili powder, and pepper. Place chicken on top of vegetables, and pour chicken broth over chicken. Cover and cook on LOW for 6 hours.

**3.** Transfer chicken to a plate, and shred with two forks into bite-size chunks; return to slow cooker. Top with tortilla strips.

# Chicken Sausage and White Bean Stew

hands-on time: 11 min. • total time: 8 hr., 11 min.
makes 4 servings

| | |
|---|---|
| 1 | (12-oz.) package spinach and feta chicken sausage, sliced |
| 3 | carrots, coarsely chopped |
| 1 | medium onion, chopped |
| ½ | tsp. salt |
| ½ | tsp. dried rosemary |
| ¼ | tsp. pepper |
| 1 | (14½-oz.) can fire-roasted diced tomatoes |
| 2 | (15.8-oz.) cans great Northern beans, undrained |
| 4 | bacon slices, cooked and crumbled |

**1.** Cook sausage in a large skillet over medium-high heat 4 minutes or until browned.

**2.** Place carrot and onion in a 4- or 5-qt. slow cooker; sprinkle with salt, rosemary, and pepper. Layer tomatoes and beans over carrot mixture. Top with sausage. Cover and cook on LOW 8 hours or until vegetables are tender. Sprinkle with bacon before serving.

## menu idea
### for 4

**Chicken Sausage and White Bean Stew**

**Spinach salad with mushrooms and onions**

**Focaccia**

## groceries needed...

Check staples: salt, dried rosemary, pepper, salad dressing

- 1 (12-oz.) package spinach and feta chicken sausage
- 1 bunch carrots
- 1 medium onion
- 1 (14½-oz.) can fire-roasted diced tomatoes
- 2 (15.8-oz.) cans great Northern beans
- 1 package bacon

## sides...

- 2 (6-oz.) packages fresh baby spinach
- 1 (8-oz.) container sliced fresh mushrooms
- 1 red onion
- 1 loaf focaccia

*groceries needed...*

Check staples, salt, pepper, olive oil

* 1½ lb. boneless lean lamb
* 2 (14.5-oz) cans diced tomatoes with garlic and onion
* 2 large jalapeño peppers
* 1 (8-oz.) container refrigerated prechopped onion
* 1 garlic bulb
* 1 (32-oz.) container plus 1 (14-oz.) can chicken broth
* 1 (15-oz.) jar creamy peanut butter
* 1 (6-oz.) can tomato paste
* 1 (24-oz.) package steam-and-mash frozen cut sweet potatoes (we tested with Ore-Ida)
* 1 (16-oz.) package frozen cut okra
* 1 bunch fresh parsley (optional)

*sides...*

* 2 (10-oz.) packages couscous
* 1 melon

*Ingredient Secret:* We used frozen cut sweet potatoes to eliminate the time-consuming task of peeling and cubing the potatoes.

# African Lamb-Peanut Stew

hands-on time: 15 min. • total time: 9 hr.
makes 10 servings

1½ lb. boneless lean lamb, cut into 1-inch pieces

1 tsp. salt, divided

¼ tsp. freshly ground pepper

2 Tbsp. olive oil

2 (14.5-oz) cans diced tomatoes with garlic and onion, undrained

2 large jalapeño peppers, minced

1 (8-oz.) container refrigerated prechopped onion

2 garlic cloves, minced

5 cups chicken broth

¾ cup creamy peanut butter

2 Tbsp. tomato paste

1 (24-oz.) package steam-and-mash frozen cut sweet potatoes

2 cups frozen cut okra

Hot cooked couscous

Garnish: chopped fresh parsley

**1.** Sprinkle lamb with ½ tsp. salt and ¼ tsp. pepper. Cook lamb in hot oil in a large skillet over medium-high heat, stirring often, 5 minutes or until browned on all sides. Drain. Place in a 6-qt. slow cooker.

**2.** Add tomatoes and next 3 ingredients to slow cooker. Whisk together broth, remaining ½ tsp. salt, peanut butter, and tomato paste; pour over vegetables and lamb. Cover and cook on LOW 8 hours. Stir in sweet potatoes and okra. Cook 45 more minutes or until vegetables are tender. Serve over couscous. Garnish, if desired.

*ideal slow cooker:*

5-quart

*menu idea*

**for 8 to 10 servings**

Irish Lamb Stew

Irish soda bread

# Irish Lamb Stew

hands-on time: 13 min. • total time: 7 hr., 33 min.
makes 8 to 10 servings

| | |
|---|---|
| 3 | center-cut bacon slices |
| 2 | lb. boneless lean lamb, cut into ½-inch pieces |
| 1 | tsp. salt |
| ½ | tsp. freshly ground pepper |
| ¾ | cup (¼-inch-thick) carrot slices |
| ½ | cup diced celery |
| 3 | garlic cloves, minced |
| 2 | (14-oz.) cans beef broth |
| 1 | lb. small round red potatoes, quartered |
| 1 | small onion, cut into thin wedges |
| ¼ | cup cornstarch |

Chopped fresh marjoram

**1.** Cook bacon in a large skillet over medium-high heat 4 to 5 minutes or until crisp; remove bacon, and drain on paper towels, reserving drippings in skillet. Coarsely crumble bacon.

**2.** Sprinkle lamb with salt and pepper; add to drippings in skillet. Cook lamb 5 minutes or until browned on all sides, stirring occasionally. Stir in 2 cups water, stirring to loosen particles from bottom of skillet. Transfer lamb mixture to a 5-qt. slow cooker. Stir in crumbled bacon, carrot, and next 5 ingredients. Cover and cook on LOW 7 hours or until lamb is tender.

**3.** Increase slow cooker temperature to HIGH. Combine cornstarch and 3 tablespoons water in a small bowl, stirring until smooth. Stir cornstarch mixture into stew. Cover and cook 20 minutes or until slightly thickened, stirring occasionally. Ladle stew into bowls; sprinkle with marjoram.

*groceries needed...*

Check staples: salt, pepper, cornstarch

* 1 package center-cut bacon
* 2 lb. boneless lean lamb
* 1 bunch carrots
* 1 bunch celery
* 1 garlic bulb
* 2 (14-oz.) cans beef broth
* 1 lb. small round red potatoes
* 1 small onion
* 1 bunch fresh marjoram

*side...*

* 1 loaf Irish soda bread

menu idea
for 8

**Easy Brunswick Stew**

**Cornsticks**

groceries needed...

Check staples: brown sugar, salt

* 3 lb. boneless pork shoulder roast (Boston Butt)
* 2 medium-size new potatoes
* 1 large onion
* 1 (28-oz.) can crushed tomatoes
* 1 (18-oz.) bottle barbecue sauce
* 1 (14-oz.) can chicken broth
* 1 (9-oz.) package frozen baby lima beans
* 1 (9-oz.) package frozen corn

sides...

* Bakery cornsticks or boxed cornbread mix

**Slow-Cooker Secret:** Cooking on low heat for a long time makes the meat extremely tender, so it shreds easily. High heat yields a less tender product.

# Easy Brunswick Stew

hands-on time: 15 min. • total time: 10 hr., 15 min.
makes 8 servings

| | |
|---|---|
| 3 | lb. boneless pork shoulder roast (Boston butt) |
| 2 | medium-size new potatoes, peeled and chopped |
| 1 | large onion, chopped |
| 1 | (28-oz.) can crushed tomatoes |
| 1 | (18-oz.) bottle barbecue sauce |
| 1 | (14-oz.) can chicken broth |
| 1 | (9-oz.) package frozen baby lima beans, thawed |
| 1 | (9-oz.) package frozen corn, thawed |
| 6 | Tbsp. brown sugar |
| 1 | tsp. salt |

**1.** Trim roast, and cut into 2-inch pieces. Stir together all ingredients in a 6-qt. slow cooker.

**2.** Cover and cook on LOW 10 hours or until potatoes are fork-tender. Remove pork with a slotted spoon, and shred with two forks. Return shredded pork to slow cooker, and stir well. Ladle stew into bowls.

**Slow-Cooker Secret: Crushing some of the beans at the end of cooking slightly thickens the chili and gives it more body and a creamy texture.**

*ideal slow cooker:*

4-quart

# Spicy Chicken Chili Verde

hands-on time: 8 min. • total time: 10 hr., 8 min.
makes 6 servings

1   lb. skinned and boned chicken thighs, cut into 1-inch pieces
1   Tbsp. vegetable oil
1   (8-oz.) container refrigerated prechopped onion
1   Tbsp. jarred minced garlic
2   cups chicken broth
1   cup salsa verde
1   cup frozen whole kernel corn
1   tsp. ground cumin
1   tsp. hot sauce
½   tsp. pepper
1   (15.5-oz.) can cannellini beans, drained

**1.** Cook chicken in hot oil in a medium skillet over medium-high heat 4 minutes or until browned, stirring often. Transfer chicken to a 4-qt. slow cooker. Add onion and garlic to drippings in skillet; sauté until vegetables are tender. Add broth, stirring to loosen particles from bottom of skillet. Add broth mixture to chicken in slow cooker. Stir in salsa and next 4 ingredients. Cover and cook on LOW 10 hours.

**2.** Add beans. Mash beans in soup with a potato masher or back of a spoon until desired consistency.

*menu idea*
for 6

Spicy Chicken
Chili Verde

Jalapeño corn muffins

Grilled pineapple
slices

*groceries needed...*

Check staples: vegetable oil, jarred minced garlic, ground cumin, hot sauce, pepper

* 1 lb. skinned and boned chicken thighs
* 1 (8-oz.) container refrigerated prechopped onion
* 1 (14-oz.) can chicken broth
* 1 (7-oz.) can salsa verde
* 1 (16-oz.) package frozen whole kernel corn
* 1 (15.5-oz.) can cannellini beans

*sides...*

* Deli jalapeño corn muffins or boxed corn muffin mix
* 1 large pineapple

*groceries needed...*

Check staples: chili powder, pepper, paprika

* 3¼ lb. ground chuck
* 1 medium-size green bell pepper
* 3 (14½-oz.) cans diced tomatoes with garlic and onion
* 3 (10¾-oz.) cans tomato soup
* 1 (16-oz.) can light red kidney beans
* 1 (6-oz.) can tomato paste
* 1 (8-oz.) container sour cream
* 1 (8-oz.) package shredded Cheddar cheese
* 1 bunch green onions
* 1 (2.25-oz.) can sliced black olives
* 1 (9.25-oz.) package corn chips

*side...*

* 2 pt. deli coleslaw

**Slow-Cooker Secret: Freeze any leftovers for a great make-ahead cold-weather comfort dish. Omit the beans, if desired.**

# Game Day Chili

hands-on: 12 min. • total time: 4 hr., 12 min.
makes 8 servings

3¼ lb. ground chuck

1 medium-size green bell pepper, chopped

3 (14½-oz.) cans diced tomatoes with garlic and onion, undrained

3 (10¾-oz.) cans tomato soup

1 (16-oz.) can light red kidney beans, rinsed and drained

1 (6-oz.) can tomato paste

5 Tbsp. chili powder

1 tsp. freshly ground pepper

½ tsp. paprika

Toppings: sour cream, shredded Cheddar cheese, chopped green onions, sliced black olives, corn chips

1. Cook ground chuck in a large nonstick skillet over medium-high heat 12 to 14 minutes or until meat crumbles and is no longer pink; drain.

2. Place meat in a 5- to 6-qt. slow cooker; stir in ½ cup water, green bell pepper, and next 7 ingredients. Cover and cook on HIGH 4 hours. Serve with desired toppings.

*ideal slow cooker:*
**4- to 5-quart**

# Cincinnati 5-Way Chili

**hands-on time: 13 min.** • **total time: 6 hr., 17 min.**
**makes 4 servings**

1½ lb. ground sirloin

1 large onion, chopped

2 garlic cloves, minced

2 Tbsp. chili powder

1½ Tbsp. unsweetened cocoa

1 Tbsp. cider vinegar

1 Tbsp. Worcestershire sauce

1 tsp. ground allspice

1 tsp. ground cinnamon

½ tsp. salt

¼ tsp. ground red pepper

1 bay leaf

1 (12-oz.) bottle German beer

1 (6-oz.) can tomato paste

Hot cooked spaghetti

Shredded sharp Cheddar cheese

Diced onion

1 (15-oz.) can kidney beans, rinsed and drained

**1.** Cook beef, onion, and garlic in a large nonstick skillet coated with cooking spray over medium-high heat 8 minutes or until browned. Stir in chili powder, next 10 ingredients, and ½ cup water. Transfer chili mixture to a 4- to 5-qt. slow cooker. Cover and cook on LOW 6 hours. Discard bay leaf.

**2.** Serve chili over hot cooked pasta. Top with cheese, diced onion, and kidney beans.

*menu idea*
**for 4**

Cincinnati 5-Way Chili
Oyster crackers
Mixed salad greens

*groceries needed...*

Check staples: chili powder, cider vinegar, Worcestershire sauce, allspice, cinnamon, salt, ground red pepper, bay leaves, salad dressing

✳ 1½ lb. ground sirloin

✳ 2 large onions

✳ 1 garlic bulb

✳ 1 (8-oz.) can unsweetened cocoa

✳ 1 (12-oz.) bottle German beer (we tested with Beck's Ocktoberfest)

✳ 1 (6-oz.) can tomato paste

✳ 1 (7-oz) package spaghetti

✳ 1 (8-oz.) package shredded sharp Cheddar cheese

✳ 1 (15-oz.) can kidney beans

*sides...*

✳ 1 (10-oz.) package oyster crackers

✳ 1 (5-oz.) bag mixed salad greens

*menu idea*
**for 8**

Tomatillo-Mushroom
Chili

Corn chips

*groceries needed...*
Check staples: extra virgin olive oil,
chili powder, ground cumin

* 6 tomatillos
* 2 onions
* 1 garlic bulb
* 1 lb. shiitake mushrooms
* 1 (32-oz.) package organic
  vegetable broth (we tested with
  Swanson)
* 2 (15-oz.) cans black beans
* 1 (14.5-oz.) can fire-roasted diced
  tomatoes
* 1 (8-oz.) package shredded
  Cheddar cheese (optional)
* 1 bunch green onions (optional)

*side...*
* 1 bag corn chips

**Ingredient Secret: Store tomatillos in a paper bag in the refrigerator for up to one month.**

# Tomatillo-Mushroom Chili

hands-on time: 10 min. • total time: 3 hr., 17 min.
makes 8 servings

1   Tbsp. extra virgin olive oil
6   tomatillos, husks removed and coarsely chopped
2   onions, coarsely chopped
2   garlic cloves, minced
1   lb. shiitake mushrooms, stems removed and coarsely chopped
2   Tbsp. chili powder
1   tsp. ground cumin
3   cups organic vegetable broth
2   (15-oz.) cans black beans, drained
1   (14.5-oz.) can fire-roasted diced tomatoes

Garnishes: shredded Cheddar cheese, chopped green onions

1. Heat a large skillet over medium-high heat; add oil. Sauté tomatillos, onion, and garlic in hot oil 7 minutes or until tender. Add mushrooms, chili powder, and cumin; sauté 3 minutes.

2. Transfer vegetable mixture to a 5-qt. slow cooker; stir in broth and next 2 ingredients. Cover and cook on LOW 3 hours. Garnish, if desired.

# {quick-fix sandwiches}

### Dressed-Up Chicken Salad

Mix deli chicken salad with halved red grapes, toasted pecans, and lettuce leaves, and serve on toasted bakery multi-grain bread.

### Olive 'n' Apple Pimiento Grilled Cheese

Add ½ cup each chopped pimiento-stuffed olives and shredded Braeburn apple to 3 cups of your favorite pimiento cheese. Slather it on bread, and cook it on a griddle (or just enjoy as a chilled spread).

## Petite Turkey Sandwiches

Use already baked Sister Schubert rolls. Stuff with deli turkey, a little bacon, and honey mustard. Butter the outsides of rolls. Gently mash each sandwich flat with a spatula as you cook it on a griddle (as you would make a grilled cheese).

# casual entertaining

When company's coming, nothing's easier than pulling out your slow cooker for delicious main dishes in a hurry. **Feed a crowd with Slow-Cooker Sloppy Joes, Sweet-and-Spicy Baby Back Ribs, or Ruby Port-Glazed Ham With Dried Fruit Sauce.** Quick and easy prep make it a snap to spend time with friends and family over a tasty meal instead of spending all day in the kitchen.

**Shopping Secret: Although many butchers label this particular cut of meat as "London broil," thick top round steak is also a common term.**

# Onion-Encrusted London Broil

**hands-on time: 4 min. • total time: 9 hr., 4 min.**
**makes 5 servings**

1   cup soft, fresh breadcrumbs
1   Tbsp. dried parsley flakes
1   tsp. freshly ground pepper
1   (1-oz.) envelope dry onion soup mix
2½  lb. London broil (at least 2 inches thick)

1. Combine first 4 ingredients in a small bowl. Press crumb mixture onto steak, coating completely. Place steak in a 4-qt. slow cooker. Cover and cook on HIGH 1 hour. Reduce heat to LOW, and cook 8 hours. Slice steak across the grain to serve.

*ideal slow cooker:*
4-quart

*menu idea*
**for 5**

Onion-Encrusted
London Broil

Roasted baby carrots
and new potatoes

Hard rolls

*groceries needed...*
Check staples: pepper
* 1 loaf fresh bread
* 1 (1-oz.) jar dried parsley flakes
* 1 (1-oz.) envelope dry onion soup mix
* 2½ lb. London broil

*sides...*
* 1½ lb. baby carrots
* 1½ lb. new potatoes
* 1 package hard rolls

# Beef and Chicken Fajitas

hands-on time: 15 min. • total time: 7 hr., 15 min.
makes 10 servings

1½  lb. flat-iron steak, cut into strips

1    lb. skinned and boned chicken breasts, cut into strips

1    tsp. salt

1    tsp. pepper

1½  Tbsp. fajita seasoning, divided

¼   cup olive oil, divided

3    Tbsp. fresh lime juice

2    Tbsp. Worcestershire sauce

5    large garlic cloves, minced

1½  (1-lb.) packages frozen pepper stir-fry

10   (8-inch) flour tortillas, warmed

Lime wedges (optional)

Toppings: guacamole, shredded lettuce, chopped tomato,
    shredded Cheddar cheese

**1.** Place steak and chicken strips on separate plates; sprinkle
with salt, pepper, and 1 Tbsp. fajita seasoning.

**2.** Heat 1 Tbsp. oil in an extra-large skillet over medium-high
heat. Add steak to pan; cook 3 minutes or until browned,
turning once. Place steak in a 5- or 6-qt. slow cooker. Add
chicken to pan; cook over medium-high heat 3 minutes or until
browned, stirring once. Add chicken to steak in slow cooker.

**3.** Stir together remaining 3 Tbsp. oil, lime juice, Worcestershire sauce, garlic and remaining 1½ tsp. fajita seasoning in
a medium bowl; pour over chicken and steak in slow cooker.
Cover and cook on LOW 5 hours or until meat is tender. Stir in
frozen pepper stir-fry. Cover and cook 1 to 2 more hours.

**4.** Spoon filling into tortillas and, if desired, squeeze lime
wedges over filling. Serve with desired toppings.

**Slow-Cooker Secret: We brown the beef before slow-cooking to add color and enhance flavor. This mixture is also great over baked potatoes with your favorite toppings.**

*ideal slow cooker:*
**5-quart**

# Slow-Cooker Beef Tacos

hands-on time: 15 min. • total time: 8 hr., 15 min.
makes 8 servings

*menu idea*
**for 8**

**Slow-Cooker Beef Tacos**

**Refried beans**

| | |
|---|---|
| 2 | lb. boneless beef chuck roast, cut into 1-inch cubes |
| 1 | tsp. salt |
| 1 | Tbsp. vegetable oil |
| 1 | Tbsp. chili powder |
| 1 | (6-oz.) can tomato paste |
| 2 | cups beef broth |
| 1 | small white onion, sliced |
| 1 | (8-oz.) can tomato sauce |
| ½ | medium-size green bell pepper |
| 1 | tsp. ground cumin |
| ½ | tsp. pepper |
| 8 | taco shells |

Toppings: shredded Cheddar cheese, shredded lettuce, fresh salsa

1. Sprinkle beef with salt.

2. Cook beef in hot oil in a Dutch oven over medium-high heat 8 minutes or until browned on all sides. Remove beef, reserving drippings in Dutch oven. Add 1 Tbsp. chili powder to Dutch oven; cook, stirring constantly, 1 minute. Stir in tomato paste, and cook, stirring constantly, 2 minutes. Add 2 cups beef broth, stirring to loosen particles from bottom of Dutch oven. Return beef to Dutch oven, and stir.

3. Place beef mixture in a 5-qt. slow cooker. Add onion and next 4 ingredients. Cook on LOW 8 hours or until beef is tender. Serve with taco shells and desired toppings.

*groceries needed...*
Check staples: salt, vegetable oil, chili powder, ground cumin, pepper
* 2 lb. boneless beef chuck roast
* 1 (6-oz.) can tomato paste
* 1 (14-oz.) can beef broth
* 1 small white onion
* 1 (8-oz.) can tomato sauce
* 1 medium-size green bell pepper
* 8 taco shells
* 1 (8-oz.) package shredded Cheddar cheese
* 1 (8-oz.) package shredded lettuce
* 1 (18-oz.) container fresh salsa

*side...*
* 2 (16-oz.) cans refried beans

*menu idea*

**for 8**

**Slow-Cooker
Sloppy Joes**

**Chips**

**Dill pickle spears**

*groceries needed...*

Check staples: ketchup, brown sugar,
cider vinegar, yellow mustard, chili
powder, Worcestershire sauce, salt,
flour

* 1½ lb. lean ground beef
* 1 (16-oz.) package ground pork
  sausage
* 1 small onion
* 1 medium-size green bell pepper
* 1 (8-oz.) can tomato sauce
* 8 hamburger buns, toasted

*sides...*

* 1 bag chips
* 1 jar dill pickle spears

**Freezing Secret: To freeze leftover sloppy joe mixture, let cool completely. Place in zip-top plastic freezer bags; lay bags flat, and stack in freezer. Freeze up to 1 month. Thaw overnight in the fridge, or defrost in the microwave.**

# Slow-Cooker Sloppy Joes

hands-on: 14 min.  •  total time: 4 hr., 14 min.
makes 8 servings

1½  lb. lean ground beef

1  (16-oz.) package ground pork sausage

1  small onion, chopped

½  medium-size green bell pepper, chopped

1  (8-oz.) can tomato sauce

½  cup ketchup

¼  cup firmly packed brown sugar

2  Tbsp. cider vinegar

2  Tbsp. yellow mustard

1  Tbsp. chili powder

1  Tbsp. Worcestershire sauce

½  tsp. salt

¼  cup all-purpose flour

8  hamburger buns, toasted

**1.** Brown beef and sausage with onion and bell pepper in a large Dutch oven over medium-high heat, stirring 10 minutes or until beef and sausage crumble and are no longer pink. Drain well.

**2.** Place beef mixture in a 4-qt. slow cooker. Stir in tomato sauce, ½ cup water, and next 8 ingredients. Cover and cook on HIGH 4 hours. Serve on hamburger buns.

**Make-Ahead Secret: Serve 1 roast now and freeze the other. Shred the roast and store it with 2 cups vegetable-and–gravy mixture in separate airtight containers in refrigerator up to 3 days or freeze up to 2 months. Each roast will serve 6 to 8.**

# Italian Company Pot Roast

hands-on time: 15 min • total time: 8 hr., 15 min.
makes 8 to 12 servings

| | |
|---|---|
| 2 | (2¼- to 2½-lb.) eye-of-round roasts, trimmed |
| 2 | tsp. salt |
| 1 | tsp. freshly ground black pepper |
| 1 | Tbsp. vegetable oil |
| 1 | (1-lb.) package baby carrots |
| 1 | (14.5-oz.) can petite diced tomatoes |
| 1 | cup chopped celery |
| 1 | cup beef broth |
| ½ | cup dry red wine |
| 4 | garlic cloves, chopped |
| 1 | tsp. dried thyme leaves |
| ½ | tsp. dried marjoram |
| ¼ | cup all-purpose flour |

1. Rub roasts evenly with 2 tsp. salt and 1 tsp. pepper.

2. Brown roasts on all sides in hot oil in a Dutch oven over medium-high heat (about 10 minutes). Place roasts, side by side, in a 6-qt. slow cooker. Add carrots and next 7 ingredients.

3. Cover and cook on LOW 8 hours or until tender. To make gravy, transfer roasts and vegetables to a serving platter; measure drippings, and return to slow cooker. For every cup of drippings, add 1 Tbsp. flour to ¼ cup water. Whisk together flour and water. Whisk mixture into drippings. Cook, uncovered, on HIGH 5 minutes.

---

*ideal slow cooker:*
6-quart

*menu idea*
**for 6 to 8**

**Italian Company Pot Roast**

**Mashed potatoes**

**Steamed peas**

*groceries needed...*

Check staples: salt, black pepper, vegetable oil, dried thyme leaves, dried marjoram, flour

* 2 (2¼- to 2½-lb.) eye-of-round roasts
* 1 (1-lb.) package baby carrots
* 1 (14.5-oz.) can petite diced tomatoes
* 1 bunch celery
* 1 (14-oz.) can beef broth
* 1 bottle dry red wine
* 1 garlic bulb

*sides...*

* 1 (32-oz.) container refrigerated mashed potatoes
* 2 (12-oz.) packages frozen sweet peas

*menu idea*

**for 6**

**Osso Buco**

**Hot cooked polenta**

**Asparagus**

*groceries needed...*

Check staples: olive oil, salt, pepper, flour

* 1 (8-oz.) container refrigerated prechopped celery, onion, and bell pepper mix
* 1 bunch carrots
* 1 garlic bulb
* 6 (1½- to 2-inch-thick) veal shanks (about 4 lb.)
* 1 bottle dry white wine
* 2 (14.5-oz.) cans diced tomatoes with basil, garlic, and oregano
* 1 (14-oz.) can beef broth
* 1 bunch fresh parsley (optional)

*sides...*

* 1 or 2 (18-oz.) tubes polenta
* 1 large bunch asparagus

# Osso Buco

hands-on time: 12 min. • total time: 8 hr., 12 min.
makes 6 servings

2 Tbsp. olive oil, divided
1 (8-oz.) container refrigerated prechopped celery, onion, and bell pepper mix
½ cup chopped carrot
3 garlic cloves, minced
6 (1½- to 2-inch-thick) veal shanks (about 4 lb.)
1 tsp. salt, divided
½ tsp. freshly ground pepper
¾ cup all-purpose flour, divided
½ cup dry white wine
2 (14.5-oz.) cans diced tomatoes with basil, garlic, and oregano
1 (14-oz.) can beef broth
**Hot cooked polenta**
**Chopped fresh parsley (optional)**

**1.** Heat 1 Tbsp. oil in a large skillet over medium-high heat. Add celery mix and carrot; sauté 3 minutes or until tender. Add garlic; sauté 1 minute or until tender. Transfer vegetable mixture to a lightly greased 5- or 6-qt. slow cooker.

**2.** Sprinkle veal with ½ tsp. salt and pepper. Dredge veal in ½ cup plus 1 Tbsp. flour; shake off excess. Heat remaining 1 Tbsp. oil in skillet over medium-high heat. Add veal; cook 3 to 4 minutes on each side or until browned. Arrange veal over vegetables in slow cooker. Add wine to drippings in skillet, stirring to loosen particles from bottom of skillet. Stir in tomatoes, broth, remaining 3 Tbsp. flour, and remaining ½ teaspoon salt. Pour over veal in slow cooker.

**3.** Cover and cook on LOW 8 hours or until veal is very tender (meat will fall off the bone). Cover and set aside until ready to serve. Serve over polenta. Sprinkle with parsley, if desired.

**Slow-Cooker Secret:** The unpeeled garlic cloves become very tender and creamy while cooking. They will slip easily out of the peels with a gentle squeeze at the root end.

# Garlic Lamb Shanks With Tomato Gravy

hands-on time: 15 min. • total time: 10 hr., 15 min.
makes 4 servings

| | |
|---|---|
| 1 | Tbsp. olive oil |
| 4 | lamb shanks (4 lb.), trimmed |
| 1 | cup dry white wine |
| 2 | Tbsp. honey |
| 2 | Tbsp. coarse-grained mustard |
| 1 | Tbsp. fresh thyme leaves |
| 1 | Tbsp. lemon zest |
| 1 | tsp. salt |
| ½ | tsp. freshly ground pepper |
| 1 | (14½-oz.) can stewed tomatoes |
| 4 | garlic bulbs, unpeeled and separated into cloves |
| 2 | Tbsp. chopped fresh parsley |

**1.** Heat oil in a large skillet over medium-high heat. Brown lamb 4 minutes on each side. Transfer lamb to a 6-qt. slow cooker. Add wine and next 8 ingredients to skillet, stirring to loosen particles from bottom of skillet. Bring to a boil; pour over lamb.

**2.** Cover and cook on LOW 10 hours or until lamb is very tender. Sprinkle with parsley before serving.

*ideal slow cooker:*
6-quart

*menu idea*
for 4

Garlic Lamb Shanks With Tomato Gravy

Couscous

Crusty bread

*groceries needed...*

Check staples: olive oil, honey, coarse-grained mustard, salt, pepper

❋ 4 lamb shanks (4 lb.)
❋ 1 bottle dry white wine
❋ 1 bunch fresh thyme leaves
❋ 1 lemon
❋ 1 (14½-oz.) can stewed tomatoes
❋ 4 garlic bulbs
❋ 1 bunch fresh parsley

*sides...*

❋ 1 (5.9-oz.) box of couscous
❋ 1 loaf crusty bread

*menu idea*

**for 4**

**Pork Carnita Nachos**

**Guacamole salad**

*groceries needed...*

Check staples: salt, pepper, vegetable oil

✳ 1 onion, sliced

✳ 1 (7-oz.) can chipotle peppers in adobo sauce

✳ 2 or 4 jalapeño peppers

✳ 2 to 3 lb. boned pork butt or shoulder

✳ 1 garlic bulb

✳ 1 (16-oz.) bag tortilla chips

✳ 1 (8-oz.) package shredded Monterey Jack cheese

✳ 1 (16-oz.) jar salsa verde

✳ 1 (18-oz.) package fresh salsa

*side...*

✳ 1 (8-oz.) package shredded iceberg lettuce

✳ 1 pt. prepared guacamole

**Serving Secret: The pork also tastes great served as tacos in flour and corn tortillas.**

# Pork Carnita Nachos

**hands-on time: 10 min. • total time: 6 hr., 10 min.**

**makes 4 servings**

1  onion, sliced

2  Tbsp. chopped canned chipotle peppers in adobo sauce or 2 fresh jalapeño peppers, seeded and sliced

2  to 3 lb. boned pork butt or shoulder

4  garlic cloves, slivered

Salt and pepper

1  Tbsp. vegetable oil

Tortilla chips

Toppings: jalapeños, shredded Monterey Jack cheese, salsa verde, fresh salsa

**1.** Combine onion, chipotle peppers, and ¼ cup water in a 5-qt. slow cooker. Using a knife, make slits all over pork, and insert garlic. Season roast with salt and pepper. Heat a large Dutch oven over medium-high heat; add oil. Brown roast on all sides, about 8 minutes. Transfer roast to slow cooker. Pour ½ cup water into pan, stirring over low heat, using a wooden spoon, to loosen browned particles from bottom of Dutch oven. Pour liquid into slow cooker. Cover and cook on HIGH for 6 hours.

**2.** Remove roast from slow cooker; let cool. Shred pork, using two forks. Return pulled pork to slow cooker, stirring to combine. Serve pork over tortilla chips with desired toppings.

*ideal slow cooker:*
7-quart oval

# Sweet-and-Spicy Baby Back Ribs

hands-on time: 15 min. • total time: 8 hr., 15 min.
makes 8 servings

2    slabs baby back ribs (about 5 lb.), halved
3    green onions, chopped
1    Tbsp. minced fresh ginger
1½   tsp. jarred minced garlic
1    Tbsp. vegetable oil
1    (12-oz.) bottle chili sauce
1    (8-oz.) bottle hoisin sauce
½    cup applesauce
½    cup beer
2    Tbsp. Worcestershire sauce
1    Tbsp. country-style Dijon mustard
1    to 3 tsp. hot sauce

**1.** Preheat broiler with oven rack 5½ inches from heat. Coat the rack of a broiler pan and broiler pan with cooking spray. Place ribs on rack in broiler pan. Broil 10 minutes.

**2.** Meanwhile, sauté green onion, ginger, and garlic in hot oil in a small saucepan over medium heat 3 to 5 minutes or until tender. Stir in chili sauce and next 6 ingredients. Bring to a boil; reduce heat to medium-low, and simmer 5 minutes.

**3.** Arrange half of ribs in a single layer in a lightly greased 7-qt. oval slow cooker. Pour half of sauce mixture over ribs. Top with remaining ribs in a single layer. Pour remaining sauce mixture over ribs. Cover and cook on LOW 4 hours or until tender. Transfer to a serving platter.

*menu idea*
for 4 to 6

**Sweet-and-Spicy Baby Back Ribs**

**Coleslaw**

**Baked beans**

*groceries needed...*

Check staples: jarred minced garlic, vegetable oil, Worcestershire sauce, hot sauce

❋ 2 slabs baby back ribs (about 5 lb.)
❋ 1 bunch green onions
❋ 1 piece fresh ginger
❋ 1 (12-oz.) bottle chili sauce
❋ 1 (8-oz.) bottle hoisin sauce
❋ 1 (23-oz.) jar applesauce
❋ 1 bottle beer
❋ 1 (6-oz.) jar country-style Dijon mustard

*sides...*

❋ 1½ pt. deli coleslaw
❋ 1½ pt. deli baked beans

*groceries needed...*

Check staples: kosher salt, pepper, salad dressing

* 2 medium onions
* 1 garlic bulb
* 6 small carrots
* 2 small parsnips
* 1 oz. dried porcini mushrooms
* 1 (8.5-oz.) jar sun-dried tomatoes
* 1 small bunch sage
* 5 lb. short ribs
* 1 bottle red wine
* 1 bunch fresh sage leaves (optional)

*sides...*

* 1 loaf crusty French bread
* 2 (8-oz.) packages mixed salad greens

**Serving Secret: You can also serve this hearty recipe over mashed potatoes or polenta.**

# Red Wine-Braised Short Ribs

hands-on time: 10 min. • total time: 8 hr., 10 min.
makes 6 servings

2   medium onions, cut into wedges

4   garlic cloves, peeled and crushed

6   small carrots, peeled and cut in half crosswise

2   small parsnips, peeled and cut in quarters crosswise

1   oz. dried porcini mushrooms, rinsed

1   (8.5-oz.) jar sun-dried tomatoes, drained and cut in half lengthwise

1   small bunch sage

5   lb. short ribs

1½  tsp. kosher salt

¾   tsp. pepper

1   bottle red wine

Garnish: fresh sage leaves

**1.** Combine onion, garlic, carrots, parsnips, mushrooms, tomatoes, and sage in a 6-qt. slow cooker. Season short ribs with 1½ tsp. salt and ¾ tsp. pepper, and nestle them among vegetables. Add wine. Cover and cook on HIGH 8 hours or until meat is tender and falls from the bones. Using a large spoon, skim off excess fat and discard. Divide ribs and vegetables among shallow bowls, and spoon sauce over top. Garnish, if desired.

## Slow-Cooker Pork Butt Roast

hands-on time: 8 min. • total time: 8 hr., 8 min.
makes 8 to 10 servings

1   (4-lb.) boneless pork shoulder roast (Boston butt)
4   Tbsp. olive oil, divided
2   tsp. salt
2   tsp. pepper
Barbecue sauce (optional)

**1.** Trim roast. Rinse roast, and pat dry. Rub roast with 1 Tbsp. olive oil. Sprinkle with salt and pepper.

**2.** Cook roast in remaining 3 Tbsp. hot oil in a large skillet over medium-high heat 2 minutes on each side or until browned. Place roast in a lightly greased 6-qt. slow cooker, fat side up.

**3.** Cover and cook on HIGH 1 hour. Reduce heat to LOW, and cook 7 hours or until meat is tender and slices easily. Remove pork, reserving liquid; slice meat. Add 1 cup reserved liquid to pork to moisten. Drizzle with barbecue sauce, if desired.

*ideal slow cooker:*

6-quart

*menu idea*
**for 8 to 10**

**Slow-Cooker Pork Butt Roast**

**Baked beans**

**Potato salad**

*groceries needed...*

Check staples: olive oil, salt, pepper

* 1 (4-lb.) boneless pork shoulder roast
* 1 (18-oz.) bottle barbecue sauce (optional)

*sides...*

* 2 or 3 (16-oz.) cans baked beans
* 2 pt. deli potato salad

*menu idea*

**for 8 to 10**

**Honey Mustard-Glazed Ham**

**Mashed sweet potatoes**

**Green beans**

**Parker House rolls**

*groceries needed...*

Check staples: light brown sugar, honey, Dijon mustard

* 1 (7- to 7½-lb.) fully cooked, bone-in ham
* 1 (32-oz.) container apple juice
* 1 orange
* 1 bunch red grapes
* Fresh parsley

*sides...*

* 2 (24-oz.) packages refrigerated mashed sweet potatoes
* 2 lb. green beans
* 1 package Parker House rolls

**Slow-Cooker Secret: We chose the shank portion of the ham because it fits in a slow cooker better and makes a prettier presentation than the butt portion. Examine the ham carefully before purchase to make sure it isn't pre-sliced.**

# Honey Mustard-Glazed Ham

hands-on time: 6 min. • total time: 8 hr., 6 min.
makes 8 to 10 servings

1    (7- to 7½-lb.) fully cooked, bone-in ham
¾    cup firmly packed light brown sugar
¾    cup honey
½    cup Dijon mustard
¼    cup apple juice

**Garnishes: orange wedges, red grapes, fresh parsley**

1. Remove skin and excess fat from ham. Score fat on ham, 1 inch apart, in a diamond pattern. Place ham in a 6-qt. oval slow cooker.

2. Stir together brown sugar and next 3 ingredients in a small bowl. Brush brown sugar mixture over ham. Cover and cook on LOW 8 hours or until a meat thermometer registers 140°. Garnish, if desired.

> **Slow-Cooker Secret:** Stand the ham up on a side to snugly fit into the slow cooker (oval works best).

*ideal slow cooker:*

**7-quart oval**

# Ruby Port-Glazed Ham With Dried Fruit Sauce

hands-on time: 11 min. • total time: 6 hr., 26 min.
makes 12 to 14 servings

| | |
|---|---|
| 1 | (6½-lb.) fully cooked, bone-in ham (butt portion) |
| ¼ | cup stone-ground mustard |
| 1 | cup firmly packed light brown sugar |
| 1 | cup pitted whole dates |
| 1 | cup dried pitted plums |
| ½ | cup mission figlets, halved |
| 1 | cup ruby port or tawny port wine |
| ½ | cup fig preserves |

Garnish: kumquats

**1.** Remove skin from ham, and trim fat to ¼-inch thickness. Score fat on ham 1 inch apart in a diamond pattern. Place ham in a 7-qt. oval slow cooker. Brush ham with mustard. Press brown sugar firmly into mustard on ham. Sprinkle dates, plums, and figlets around ham.

**2.** Stir together port and preserves; drizzle lightly over ham and pour onto fruit. Cover and cook on LOW 6 hours, quickly spooning port mixture over ham twice during cooking.

**3.** Remove ham from slow cooker, and place on a platter; cover with aluminum foil. Transfer fruit and sauce to a large saucepan. Bring to a boil; boil 15 minutes or until sauce is thickened. Slice ham and spoon sauce over ham. Garnish, if desired.

*menu idea*
**for 12 to 14**

**Ruby Port-Glazed Ham With Dried Fruit Sauce**

**Broccolini**

**Scalloped potatoes**

**Biscuits**

*groceries needed...*

Check staples: light brown sugar

* 1 (6½-lb.) fully cooked, bone-in ham (butt portion)
* 1 (9-oz.) jar stone-ground mustard
* 1 (12-oz.) bag pitted whole dates
* 1 (10-oz.) package dried pitted plums
* 1 (8-oz.) package mission figlets (we tested with Orchard Choice)
* 1 bottle ruby port or tawny port wine
* 1 (10-oz.) jar fig preserves
* Kumquats (optional)

*sides...*

* 3 lb. fresh broccolini
* 2 (5-oz.) boxes scalloped potatoes
* 1 large bag frozen biscuits

**menu idea**
for 8

**Cheesy Scalloped Potatoes With Ham**

**Assorted fruit**

**Lemon sherbet**

*groceries needed...*

Check staples: butter, flour, salt, pepper, cooking spray

* 2 (12-oz.) cans evaporated milk
* 2 (20-oz.) packages refrigerated sliced potatoes
* 3 cups chopped cooked ham
* 1 (12-oz.) package shredded sharp Cheddar cheese
* 1 (3-oz.) package real bacon pieces (we tested with Oscar Mayer)
* 1 bunch green onions

*sides...*

* Assorted fruit
* ½ gallon lemon sherbet

**Ingredient Secret: Refrigerated sliced potatoes are a handy convenience item that eliminates the chore of peeling and thinly slicing pounds of potatoes.**

# Cheesy Scalloped Potatoes With Ham

hands-on time: 14 min. • total time: 2 hr., 54 min.
makes 8 servings

| | |
|---|---|
| 6 | Tbsp. butter, divided |
| 3 | Tbsp. all-purpose flour |
| 2¼ | cups evaporated milk |
| ¾ | tsp. salt |
| ½ | tsp. freshly ground pepper |
| 2 | (20-oz.) packages refrigerated sliced potatoes |
| 3 | cups chopped cooked ham |
| 3 | cups (12 oz.) shredded sharp Cheddar cheese |
| 1 | (3-oz.) package real bacon pieces |
| ¼ | cup chopped green onions |

**1.** Melt ¼ cup butter in a heavy saucepan over low heat; whisk in flour until smooth. Cook 1 minute, whisking constantly. Gradually whisk in milk; cook over medium heat, whisking constantly, until mixture is thickened and bubbly. Stir in salt and pepper.

**2.** Layer potatoes, white sauce, ham, and next 3 ingredients in a 5-qt. oval slow cooker coated with cooking spray. Dot with remaining 2 Tbsp. butter.

**3.** Cover and cook on HIGH 2½ hours or until potatoes are tender. Let stand 10 minutes before serving.

**Serving Secret: Shredded smoked barbecue pork flavors these baked beans and makes them the entrée. Serve beans in small ramekins on a picnic plate with the other menu items.**

# Party Pork and Beans

hands-on time: 13 min. • total time: 7 hr., 13 min.
makes 12 servings

4  fully cooked bacon slices
3  (28-oz.) cans baked beans
1  cup refrigerated prechopped onion
½  cup firmly packed brown sugar
½  cup barbecue sauce
2  Tbsp. yellow mustard
1  (20-oz.) can pineapple tidbits in juice, drained
¾  lb. smoked barbecue pork, shredded

1. Prepare bacon according to microwave directions.

2. Meanwhile, stir together beans and next 4 ingredients in a greased 4- or 5-qt. slow cooker. Add 1½ cups pineapple tidbits, reserving remaining tidbits for other uses. Gently stir in pork. Top with bacon slices.

3. Cover and cook on LOW 5 hours. Uncover and cook 2 more hours or until sauce thickens.

*ideal slow cooker:*

4- or 5-quart

*menu idea*
for 12

**Party Pork and Beans**

**Corn on the cob**

**Rolls**

*groceries needed...*

Check staples: brown sugar, yellow mustard

* 1 (2.1-oz.) package fully cooked bacon slices
* 3 (28-oz.) cans baked beans (we tested with Bush's)
* 1 (8-oz.) container refrigerated prechopped onion
* 1 (18-oz.) bottle barbecue sauce (we tested with Stubb's)
* 1 (20-oz.) can pineapple tidbits in juice
* ¾ lb. smoked barbecue pork, shredded

*sides...*

* 6 ears fresh corn
* 1 dozen bakery rolls

*menu idea*
### for 6

Huevos Rancheros

Grilled
pineapple slices

*groceries needed...*

Check staples: ground cumin, dried oregano, eggs, hot sauce

- 1 (1-lb.) package hot ground pork sausage or chorizo
- 2 (8-oz.) container refrigerated prechopped bell pepper-and-onion mix
- 1 (28-oz.) can crushed tomatoes
- 2 (16-oz.) cans pinto beans
- 10 (6-inch) corn tortillas, divided
- 2 cups (8 oz.) shredded pepper Jack or Monterey Jack cheese
- 1 (16-oz.) jar pico de gallo or chunky salsa
- 1 bunch fresh cilantro

*side...*

- 1 large pineapple

# Huevos Rancheros

hands-on time: 12 min. • total time: 3 hr., 47 min.
makes 6 servings

| | |
|---|---|
| 1 | (1-lb.) package hot ground pork sausage or chorizo |
| 2 | cups refrigerated prechopped bell pepper-and-onion mix |
| 1 | (28-oz.) can crushed tomatoes |
| 2 | (16-oz.) cans pinto beans, drained |
| 1½ | tsp. ground cumin |
| 1 | tsp. dried oregano |
| 10 | (6-inch) corn tortillas, divided |
| 6 | large eggs |
| 2 | cups (8 oz.) shredded pepper Jack or Monterey Jack cheese |
| 1 | cup pico de gallo or chunky salsa |
| ¼ | cup chopped fresh cilantro |
| 2 | tsp. chipotle hot sauce |

Garnish: fresh cilantro

**1.** Brown sausage in a large skillet over medium-high heat, stirring until meat crumbles and is no longer pink. Remove sausage from skillet using a slotted spoon; reserve drippings in skillet. Spoon sausage into a 6-qt. oval slow cooker. Sauté bell pepper mix in drippings over medium-high heat 2 minutes. Stir in tomatoes, beans, cumin, and oregano; spoon over sausage in cooker.

**2.** Meanwhile, tear 4 tortillas into pieces; stir into bean mixture in cooker. Cover and cook on HIGH 3 hours.

**3.** Make 6 indentations in top of bean mixture in slow cooker, using back of a spoon. Break eggs, one at a time, into a measuring cup; slip eggs, one at a time, into indentations. Cover and cook on HIGH 20 to 30 minutes or until eggs are desired degree of doneness. Uncover and sprinkle with cheese. Turn off cooker; cover and let stand 5 minutes. Preheat oven to 450°. Arrange remaining 6 tortillas on a large baking sheet. Coat both sides with cooking spray. Bake at 450° for 10 to 11 minutes. Stir together pico de gallo, ¼ cup cilantro, and hot sauce.

**4.** Place tortillas on a platter. Top each tortilla with bean mixture, egg, and pico de gallo mixture. Garnish, if desired.

# Sausage-Tomato Cassoulet With Crumb Topping

hands-on time: 8 min. • total time: 10 hr., 8 min.
makes 8 servings

2   lb. mild Italian sausage (about 10 links), cut into ½-inch slices
6   bacon slices, chopped
6   large firm, ripe tomatoes, cut into eighths
2   (15.5-oz.) cans cannellini beans, drained
2   Tbsp. sugar
1   tsp. dried thyme
½   tsp. salt
½   tsp. freshly ground pepper
1   bay leaf
2   (8-oz.) containers refrigerated prechopped celery, onion, and bell pepper mix
1   Tbsp. jarred minced garlic
2   cups soft, fresh breadcrumbs (about 6 bread slices)
½   cup butter, melted
Garnish: fresh thyme

**1.** Cook sausage and bacon in a large skillet over medium-high heat 7 minutes or until browned, stirring occasionally.

**2.** Meanwhile, combine tomato and next 6 ingredients in a 6-qt. slow cooker. Remove sausage mixture from skillet with a slotted spoon, reserving 2 tablespoons drippings in skillet. Stir sausage mixture into tomato mixture in slow cooker. Cook celery mix and garlic in hot drippings, stirring often, 3 minutes or until tender.

**3.** Stir celery mixture into sausage mixture. Cover and cook on LOW 10 hours.

**4.** Preheat oven to 375°. Place breadcrumbs in a medium bowl; drizzle with melted butter, and toss well. Spread crumb mixture in a single layer on a baking sheet. Bake at 375° for 10 minutes or until browned and crisp. Remove bay leaf, and serve cassoulet hot, topped with toasted crumbs. Garnish, if desired.

*ideal slow cooker:*
**6-quart**

*menu idea*
**for 8**

**Sausage-Tomato Cassoulet With Crumb Topping**

**Mixed salad greens**

**Crusty French rolls**

*groceries needed:*

Check staples: sugar, dried thyme, salt, pepper, bay leaves, jarred minced garlic, butter, salad dressing

❋ 2 lb. mild Italian sausage (about 10 links)
❋ 1 package bacon
❋ 6 large firm, ripe tomatoes
❋ 2 (15.5-oz.) cans cannellini beans
❋ 2 (8-oz.) containers refrigerated prechopped celery, onion, and bell pepper mix
❋ 1 loaf bread
❋ 1 bunch fresh thyme (optional)

*sides...*

❋ 2 or 3 bags mixed salad greens
❋ 1 package crusty French rolls

*menu idea*

**for 8**

**Easy Slow-Cooker Jambalaya**

**Crusty rolls**

*groceries needed...*

Check staples: dried thyme, dried oregano

* 2 lb. skinned and boned chicken thighs
* 1 lb. smoked sausage
* 1 (8-oz.) container refrigerated prechopped celery, onion, and bell pepper mix
* 1 (28-oz.) can diced tomatoes
* 1 garlic bulb
* 1 (14-oz.) can chicken broth
* 1 Tbsp. Cajun spice mix
* ¾ lb. extra large shrimp, peeled and deveined (1 lb. raw in shell)
* 1 (32-oz.) box converted rice
* 1 bunch fresh parsley

*side...*

* 1 package crusty rolls

**Flavor Secret: For a spicier dish, add a little bit of hot sauce.**

# Easy Slow-Cooker Jambalaya

hands-on time: 11 min. • total time: 5 hr., 41 min.
makes 8 servings

| | |
|---|---|
| 2 | lb. skinned and boned chicken thighs |
| 1 | lb. smoked sausage, cut into 2-inch slices |
| 1 | (8-oz.) container refrigerated prechopped celery, onion, and bell pepper mix |
| 1 | (28-oz.) can diced tomatoes, undrained |
| 3 | garlic cloves, chopped |
| 2 | cups chicken broth |
| 1 | Tbsp. Cajun spice mix |
| 1 | tsp. dried thyme |
| 1 | tsp. dried oregano |
| ¾ | lb. extra large raw shrimp, peeled and deveined |
| 1¾ | cups converted rice |

Garnish: chopped parsley

1. Combine chicken, sausage, celery mix, tomatoes, garlic, chicken broth, spice mix, thyme, and oregano in a 5-qt. slow cooker. Cook on LOW for 5 hours.

2. Add shrimp and rice; increase heat to HIGH, and cook for 30 minutes. Sprinkle with chopped parsley, if desired.

# Paella

**hands-on time: 12 min.** • **total time: 2 hr., 30 min.**
**makes 8 servings**

3   (5-oz.) packages yellow rice
1   lb. chorizo sausage, cut diagonally into ½-inch slices
3   cups pulled deli-roasted chicken
1   (8-oz.) container refrigerated prechopped tricolor bell pepper
1   (5.75-oz.) jar pimiento-stuffed Spanish olives, drained
1   (8-oz.) container refrigerated prechopped onion
1   tsp. jarred minced garlic
1   (14.5-oz) can diced tomatoes, undrained
¾   lb. unpeeled, medium-size raw shrimp
1   cup frozen English peas

**1.** Place rice in bottom of a lightly greased 5-qt. slow cooker. Sauté chorizo in a large skillet over medium-high heat 4 minutes or until browned. Remove sausage from skillet with a slotted spoon, reserving 2 Tbsp. drippings in pan. Layer sausage, chicken, and next 2 ingredients over rice.

**2.** Sauté onion and garlic in hot drippings 3 minutes or until lightly browned. Add 4 cups water and tomatoes, stirring to loosen particles from bottom of skillet. Bring to a boil; remove from heat. Pour onion mixture over chicken mixture in slow cooker. (Do not stir.) Cover and cook on LOW 2 hours.

**3.** Meanwhile, peel shrimp, leaving tails intact.

**4.** Increase temperature to HIGH. Add shrimp and peas to slow cooker. Cover and cook 15 minutes or until shrimp turn pink.

*ideal slow cooker:*
**5-quart**

*menu idea*
**for 8**
**Paella**
**Garlic bread**

*groceries needed...*
Check staples: jarred minced garlic

❋ 3 (5-oz.) packages yellow rice
❋ 1 lb. chorizo sausage
❋ 1 deli-roasted chicken
❋ 1 (8-oz.) container refrigerated prechopped tricolor bell pepper
❋ 1 (5.75-oz.) jar pimiento-stuffed Spanish olives
❋ 1 (8-oz.) container refrigerated prechopped onion
❋ 1 (14.5-oz) can diced tomatoes
❋ ¾ lb. unpeeled, medium-size raw shrimp
❋ 1 (12-oz.) package frozen English peas

*side...*
❋ 1 package garlic bread

*menu idea*

**for 4**

**Apple Butter-Glazed Turkey**

**Sautéed spinach**

**Parker House rolls**

*groceries needed...*

Check staples: dark brown sugar, kosher salt, cornstarch

* 2 pounds large carrots
* 4 (1-lb.) turkey tenderloins
* 1 (28-oz.) jar apple butter
* 1 (6-oz.) can frozen orange juice concentrate
* 1 (1.2-oz.) can pumpkin pie spice
* 1 orange (optional)

*sides...*

* 2 (6-oz.) packages fresh spinach, thoroughly washed
* 1 package Parker House rolls

**Slow-Cooker Secret: Boneless turkey tenderloins cook faster and don't need carving like a bone-in turkey breast.**

# Apple Butter-Glazed Turkey

hands-on time: 10 min. • total time: 6 hr., 10 min.
makes 4 servings

| | |
|---|---|
| 2 | pounds large carrots, cut into ½-inch slices |
| 4 | (1-lb.) turkey tenderloins |
| 1 | cup firmly packed dark brown sugar |
| ½ | cup apple butter |
| ¼ | cup frozen orange juice concentrate, thawed |
| 2 | tsp. pumpkin pie spice |
| 1 | tsp. kosher salt |
| 2 | Tbsp. cornstarch |

Garnish: orange zest

**1.** Place carrot in a 5-qt. slow cooker. Arrange turkey on top of carrot.

**2.** Combine brown sugar and next 4 ingredients. Pour mixture over turkey tenderloins. Cover and cook on HIGH 1 hour.

**3.** Reduce temperature to LOW, and cook 5 hours or until turkey and carrot are tender.

**4.** Place turkey and carrot on a serving platter. Pour juices through a wire mesh strainer into a 3-qt. saucepan. Bring to a boil. Whisk together cornstarch and 3 Tbsp. water until smooth. Gradually whisk cornstarch mixture into juices. Cook 1 minute or until thickened, whisking constantly. Serve sauce over turkey and carrots. Garnish, if desired.

# Turkey and Dressing

hands-on time: 15 min. • total time: 6 hr., 15 min.
makes 6 servings

1   (3-lb.) frozen boned skin-on turkey breast
1   (8-oz.) bag herb-seasoned stuffing mix
1½  cups refrigerated prechopped celery, onion, and
    bell pepper mix
½   cup dried apricots, coarsely chopped
½   cup dried dates, chopped
2   Tbsp. chopped fresh rosemary
¾   cup coarsely chopped pecans
¾   cup chicken broth
3   Tbsp. butter, melted
2   Tbsp. butter, softened
¼   tsp. salt
¼   tsp. pepper
1   (.88-oz.) package turkey gravy mix
Garnish: fresh rosemary

**1.** Thaw turkey breast in refrigerator, and follow basic preparation according to package directions.

**2.** Place stuffing mix and next 5 ingredients in a lightly greased 4-qt. slow cooker. Combine broth and melted butter. Pour over stuffing, stirring gently.

**3.** Rinse and pat turkey dry with paper towels. Place turkey, breast side up, over dressing. Rub softened butter over turkey breast; sprinkle with salt and pepper. Cover and cook on HIGH 1 hour. Reduce heat to LOW, and cook 5 hours or until a meat thermometer registers 170°.

**4.** Place turkey on a platter; cover with aluminum foil. Stir stuffing; cover and let stand 4 minutes.

**5.** Meanwhile, prepare gravy mix according to package directions. Spoon stuffing around turkey on platter. Serve with gravy. Garnish, if desired.

*ideal slow cooker:*
**4-quart**

*menu idea*
**for 6**

**Turkey and Dressing**
**Roasted Brussels sprouts and carrots**
**Dinner rolls**

*groceries needed...*

Check staples: butter, salt, pepper

- 1 (3-lb.) frozen boned skin-on turkey breast (we tested with Butterball)
- 1 (8-oz.) bag herb-seasoned stuffing mix (we tested with Pepperidge Farm)
- 1 (8-oz.) container refrigerated prechopped celery, onion, and bell pepper mix
- 1 (6-oz.) package dried apricots
- 1 (6-oz.) package dried dates
- 1 bunch fresh rosemary
- ¾ cup coarsely chopped pecans
- 1 (14-oz.) can chicken broth
- 1 (.88-oz.) package turkey gravy mix (we tested with McCormick)

*sides...*

- 1½ lb. fresh Brussels sprouts
- 1 (2-lb.) package carrots
- 1 package dinner rolls

**Ingredient Secret: We found that 12-oz. potatoes cooked perfectly in 6 hours and were just the right size for entrée servings.**

*ideal slow cooker:*
**6-quart**

# Crab-Stuffed Loaded Potatoes

hands-on time: 14 min. • total time: 6 hr., 14 min.
makes 6 servings

*menu idea*
for 6

Crab-Stuffed
Loaded Potatoes

Tossed salad

| | |
|---|---|
| 6 | (12-oz.) baking potatoes |
| 1 | Tbsp. olive oil |
| ¼ | cup butter |
| 2 | Tbsp. drained capers |
| 8 | oz. fresh lump crabmeat, drained |
| 1 | Tbsp. mayonnaise |
| 1 | Tbsp. fresh lemon juice |

Salt and freshly ground pepper to taste

| | |
|---|---|
| ½ | cup butter, softened |
| ⅔ | cup half-and-half |
| ¼ | cup Japanese breadcrumbs (panko) |

Garnish: diagonally sliced fresh chives

1. Wash potatoes; pat dry. Pierce potatoes several times with a fork. Rub potatoes with oil; arrange in a 6-qt. slow cooker. Cover and cook on LOW 6 hours or until tender.

2. Melt ¼ cup butter in a skillet over medium-high heat. Add capers; cook until they begin to sizzle. Add crabmeat. Stir in mayonnaise and lemon juice. Season with salt and pepper to taste. Cover and set aside.

3. Remove potatoes from slow cooker. Cool to touch. Cut a thin slice off top of each potato; carefully scoop out pulp into a large bowl, leaving shells intact. Mash together pulp, ½ cup butter, and half-and-half. Season with salt and pepper to taste. Spoon potato mixture into shells. Reheat crab mixture 1 minute, if necessary. Top potatoes evenly with crab mixture. Sprinkle with toasted breadcrumbs. Garnish, if desired.

*groceries needed...*

Check staples: olive oil, butter, mayonnaise, salt, pepper, salad dressing

* 6 (12-oz.) baking potatoes
* 1 (8-oz.) package Japanese breadcrumbs (panko)
* 1 (3.5-oz.) jar capers
* 8 oz. fresh lump crabmeat
* 1 lemon
* 1 pt. half-and-half
* 1 bunch fresh chives (optional)

*side...*
* 2 (5-oz.) bags mixed salad greens

*menu idea*

**for 8**

Muffuletta Brunch
Strata

Bloody Marys

*groceries needed...*

Check staples: eggs, milk, dried Italian
seasoning

- 1 (32-oz.) jar garden mix olive
  salad (we tested with Gardinera)
- 1 (7-oz.) jar pimiento-stuffed
  Spanish olives
- 1 package slow-cooker liners
- 1 (1-lb.) peasant bread loaf
- 1 (8-oz.) package shredded
  mozzarella cheese
- 1 (8-oz.) package shredded
  provolone cheese
- 1 (4-oz.) package sliced
  mortadella
- 1 (4-oz.) package sliced Genoa
  salami

*side...*

- 1 bottle bloody Mary mix
- 1 bottle vodka
- 1 bunch celery

# Muffuletta Brunch Strata

hands-on time: 14 min. • total time: 3 hr., 39 min.
makes 8 servings

1  (32-oz.) jar garden mix olive salad, drained
1  (7-oz.) jar pimiento-stuffed Spanish olives, drained
1  slow-cooker liner
1  (1-lb.) peasant bread loaf, torn into bite-size pieces
1½ cups (6 oz.) shredded mozzarella cheese
1½ cups (6 oz.) shredded provolone cheese
1  (4-oz.) package sliced mortadella, chopped (about 1¼ cups)
1  (4-oz.) package sliced Genoa salami, chopped (about 1¼ cups)
6  large eggs
3  cups milk
1  tsp. dried Italian seasoning

**1.** Pulse olive salad in a food processor until coarsely
chopped. Transfer to a bowl. Process olives until coarsely
chopped; add to bowl, tossing to combine.

**2.** Place liner in a 5-qt. slow cooker according to manufacturer's instructions. Layer one-third of bread in bottom of liner.
Toss cheeses together in a bowl. Sprinkle bread with 1½ cups
cheese mixture. Sprinkle cheese with half of olive salad mixture, half of mortadella, and half of salami. Repeat layering
using one-third of bread, remaining cheese mixture, olive
salad mixture, mortadella, and salami. Top with remaining
one-third of bread.

**3.** Whisk eggs in a large bowl; whisk in milk and Italian seasoning. Pour egg mixture over bread in slow cooker until all
bread is moistened. (Cooker will be full.) Cover and cook
on HIGH 3 hours or until strata is puffed and set in center.
Uncover and cook 15 more minutes. Remove liner and strata
from cooker; let strata stand 10 minutes before serving.

**Slow-Cooker Secret: Prepare the topping at the same time as the bread mixture so it will be ready to sprinkle on when it's time to cook the pudding.**

*ideal slow cooker:*

6-quart

# Cinnamon-Pecan Breakfast Bread Pudding

hands-on time: 12 min. • total time: 12 hr., 42 min.
makes 5 servings

5    Tbsp. butter, divided
1    (16-oz.) loaf French bread, cut into ½-inch-thick slices
1½   cups sugar, divided
4    tsp. ground cinnamon, divided
¼    tsp. ground nutmeg
8    large eggs
3    cups half-and-half
2    Tbsp. vanilla extract
2    Tbsp. all-purpose flour
1    cup coarsely chopped pecans

1. Grease a 6-qt. slow cooker with 1 Tbsp. butter. Arrange bread slices in bottom of slow cooker. Whisk together ¾ cup sugar, 1 Tbsp. cinnamon, and nutmeg. Whisk in eggs, half-and-half, and vanilla. Pour over bread. Cover and chill at least 8 hours or up to 18 hours.

2. Whisk together remaining ¾ cup sugar, remaining 1 tsp. cinnamon, and flour in a bowl. Cut in remaining ¼ cup butter until crumbly; stir in pecans. Cover and chill until ready to use.

3. Remove bread mixture from refrigerator. Sprinkle pecan mixture over bread mixture. Cover and cook on HIGH 1 hour. Reduce temperature to LOW; cover and cook 3½ more hours or until puffed and set.

*menu idea*
for 5

**Cinnamon-Pecan Breakfast Bread Pudding**

**Crisp bacon strips**

**Orange slices**

**Coffee**

*groceries needed...*

Check staples: butter, sugar, ground cinnamon, ground nutmeg, eggs, vanilla extract, flour

* 1 (16-oz.) loaf French bread
* 1 qt. half-and-half
* 1 (4-oz.) package chopped pecans

*sides...*

* 1 package bacon
* 3 oranges
* Coffee

# {quick-fix starters}

## Keep It Simple

An artful grouping of assorted cheeses with snappy party accents is all that's needed to get your party started.

## Texas Cranberry Chutney

Drain 2 (8-oz.) cans pineapple tidbits, discarding liquid; pat dry with paper towels. Stir together pineapple, 1 (16-oz.) can whole-berry cranberry sauce, ¼ cup firmly packed brown sugar, ½ tsp. ground ginger, and ¼ tsp. salt in a medium saucepan over medium heat, and bring to a boil. Reduce heat to low, and simmer, stirring often, 5 minutes. Remove from heat; stir in 1 to 2 seeded and minced jalapeño peppers and 3 chopped green onions. Garnish with fresh rosemary.

## Ultimate Dirty Vodka Martini

Fill a cocktail shaker with crushed ice. Add 3 Tbsp. vermouth; cover with lid, and shake until thoroughly chilled. Discard vermouth, reserving ice in shaker. Add ½ cup vodka and 3 Tbsp. Spanish olive brine to ice in shaker; cover with lid, and shake until thoroughly chilled. Pour into a chilled martini glass. Serve immediately with a large pimiento-stuffed Spanish olive.

# metric equivalents

The recipes that appear in this cookbook use the standard U.S. method for measuring liquid and dry or solid ingredients (teaspoons, tablespoons, and cups). The information in the following charts is provided to help cooks outside the United States successfully use these recipes. All equivalents are approximate.

## Metric Equivalents for Different Types of Ingredients

A standard cup measure of a dry or solid ingredient will vary in weight depending on the type of ingredient. A standard cup of liquid is the same volume for any type of liquid. Use the following chart when converting standard cup measures to grams (weight) or milliliters (volume).

| Standard Cup | Fine Powder (ex. flour) | Grain (ex. rice) | Granular (ex. sugar) | Liquid Solids (ex. butter) | Liquid (ex. milk) |
|---|---|---|---|---|---|
| 1 | 140 g | 150 g | 190 g | 200 g | 240 ml |
| 3/4 | 105 g | 113 g | 143 g | 150 g | 180 ml |
| 2/3 | 93 g | 100 g | 125 g | 133 g | 160 ml |
| 1/2 | 70 g | 75 g | 95 g | 100 g | 120 ml |
| 1/3 | 47 g | 50 g | 63 g | 67 g | 80 ml |
| 1/4 | 35 g | 38 g | 48 g | 50 g | 60 ml |
| 1/8 | 18 g | 19 g | 24 g | 25 g | 30 ml |

## Useful Equivalents for Dry Ingredients by Weight

(To convert ounces to grams, multiply the number of ounces by 30.)

| | | | | |
|---|---|---|---|---|
| 1 oz | = | 1/16 lb | = | 30 g |
| 4 oz | = | 1/4 lb | = | 120 g |
| 8 oz | = | 1/2 lb | = | 240 g |
| 12 oz | = | 3/4 lb | = | 360 g |
| 16 oz | = | 1 lb | = | 480 g |

## Useful Equivalents for Length

(To convert inches to centimeters, multiply the number of inches by 2.5.)

| | | | | | | |
|---|---|---|---|---|---|---|
| 1 in | | | = | 2.5 cm | | |
| 6 in | = | 1/2 ft | = | 15 cm | | |
| 12 in | = | 1 ft | = | 30 cm | | |
| 36 in | = | 3 ft | = 1 yd | = | 90 cm | |
| 40 in | | | = | 100 cm | = | 1 m |

## Useful Equivalents for Liquid Ingredients by Volume

| | | | | | | | |
|---|---|---|---|---|---|---|---|
| 1/4 tsp | | | | | = | 1 ml | |
| 1/2 tsp | | | | | = | 2 ml | |
| 1 tsp | | | | | = | 5 ml | |
| 3 tsp | = | 1 Tbsp | | = 1/2 fl oz | = | 15 ml | |
| | | 2 Tbsp | = 1/8 cup | = 1 fl oz | = | 30 ml | |
| | | 4 Tbsp | = 1/4 cup | = 2 fl oz | = | 60 ml | |
| | | 5 1/3 Tbsp | = 1/3 cup | = 3 fl oz | = | 80 ml | |
| | | 8 Tbsp | = 1/2 cup | = 4 fl oz | = | 120 ml | |
| | | 10 2/3 Tbsp | = 2/3 cup | = 5 fl oz | = | 160 ml | |
| | | 12 Tbsp | = 3/4 cup | = 6 fl oz | = | 180 ml | |
| | | 16 Tbsp | = 1 cup | = 8 fl oz | = | 240 ml | |
| | | 1 pt | = 2 cups | = 16 fl oz | = | 480 ml | |
| | | 1 qt | = 4 cups | = 32 fl oz | = | 960 ml | |
| | | | | 33 fl oz | = | 1000 ml | |

## Useful Equivalents for Cooking/Oven Temperatures

| | Fahrenheit | Celsius | Gas Mark |
|---|---|---|---|
| Freeze water | 32° F | 0° C | |
| Room temperature | 68° F | 20° C | |
| Boil water | 212° F | 100° C | |
| Bake | 325° F | 160° C | 3 |
| | 350° F | 180° C | 4 |
| | 375° F | 190° C | 5 |
| | 400° F | 200° C | 6 |
| | 425° F | 220° C | 7 |
| | 450° F | 230° C | 8 |
| Broil | | | Grill |

# {index}